HOW TO READ THE FEDERALIST PAPERS

with a selection of useful quotations

© 2010 by The Heritage Foundation
214 Massachusetts Avenue, NE
Washington, DC 20002-4999
202.546.4400 ● *heritage.org*

All rights reserved.

Printed in the United States of America

ISBN: 978-0-89195-135-3

Cover photo © Geoffrey Clements/CORBIS
Photo is an image of "American Congressmen Meeting"
by Ernest Clifford Peixotto.

How to Read
The Federalist
Papers

with a selection of useful quotations

By Anthony A. Peacock

TABLE OF CONTENTS

PREFACE

The Federalist Papers enjoy an exalted status in our political
and intellectual life. Thomas Jefferson called them "the
best commentary on the principles of government, which ever
was written." Most commentators, liberal and conservative,
tend to agree.

Perhaps more important, the essays are a commentary on
our principles of government. They illustrate the major principles and ideas at the foundation of our political order and our
Constitution. Supreme Court Justices regularly cite *The Federalist* to support their interpretation of the Constitution, and our
elected officials recur to the essays when constitutional questions arise in their deliberations—important testaments to the
ongoing significance of the work.

The Federalist deserves its status. In the first place, it was
written by three of the greatest and most influential members
of our Founding generation.

- Alexander Hamilton, who wrote the majority of the
  papers and was the impetus for the project, was George
  Washington's chief confidant during the Revolutionary
  War, a leading member of the Constitutional Convention,
  and the first (and perhaps the most consequential) Secre-
  tary of the Treasury.
- James Madison was the principal intellectual leader of the
  Constitutional Convention and served as Secretary of

State under President Thomas Jefferson and as the fourth President of the United States. He is often called the "Father of the Constitution" and was central to the ratification of the Bill of Rights.

- John Jay was a leading diplomat of the Revolutionary period and served as the first Chief Justice of the Supreme Court.

In short, *The Federalist* is so noteworthy because it reflects the political ideas that were central to the creation of the Constitution itself.

Equally important is the proximity of *The Federalist* to the ratification debates. All of the Founders agreed that the authority of the Constitution does not come from their theories and preferences. Rather, the meaning of the Constitution comes from those who ratified it, for it is from the people that government derives its sovereignty. Therefore, for those who take as their compass the original Constitution, with its legitimately ratified amendments, it is the Constitution as it was understood by its ratifiers that matters, and *The Federalist* offers us the clearest insight into the mind of the ratifying generation.

There is a final reason that we rightfully study *The Federalist*, and it is the most important reason. The authors of *The Federalist* were not merely expounding on the text and meaning of the Constitution. They were giving a public argument about the reasons that made the Constitution worth ratifying, and in this endeavor they looked not only to the immediate necessities of 1787 and 1788, but also to future generations.

In the pages of *The Federalist*, the authors do not just look to immediate exigencies; they also consider the future prospects for America, and in doing so, they offer us their counsel for the challenges we face today. Because they understood that the principles of popular government, representation, separation of powers, and civic virtue would not always be unquestioned, they gave us the strongest defense of those principles in the midst of an immediate struggle for ratification.

Therefore, it is not merely the arguments of *The Federalist* that command our attention, but also the example of its rhetoric. The rhetoric of *The Federalist* is the rhetoric of statesmanship—of making strong rebuttals, driving to the root of things, basing one's positions on principle, and arguing immediate points while also looking to the long-term good. Those who consult *The Federalist* must not merely note the arguments contained therein. They must also absorb the tone and technique of the papers as models by which they can continue to elevate public discourse in their own time.

The following is a brief guide to *The Federalist*. It is not a substitute for reading the book, but rather a road map to help illuminate the major issues treated in the essays and explain their continued relevance for today. At the end of the monograph, an appendix of important passages on contemporary subjects is included as a useful resource for interested readers.

This publication is part of a series of occasional monographs published by The Heritage Foundation, under the auspices of the B. Kenneth Simon Center for American Studies, on the "First Principles" of the American tradition of ordered liberty that we seek to conserve "for ourselves and our posterity," as it says in our Constitution. These publications cover a range of themes and topics, each aimed at explaining our most primary ideas—which often seem to have been forgotten or rejected—and considering what those principles should mean for America today.

This series is motivated by a powerful observation: Those that lead our nation today—and those who will lead it tomorrow—must *know* and *understand* our first principles if they mean to vindicate those principles and see to it that they once again guide our country.

It is true that our contemporary system of government is in profound tension with our Constitution. Yet our author, Anthony Peacock, offers us hope. "The teaching of *The Federalist*," he writes, "was intended to be true for all times and all places." Despite the rise of a federal government with unlimited power and an administrative state where law is made and executed by unaccountable bureaucrats, we still enjoy some measure of constitutional government.

More important, our forebears have left us their teaching and example, showing us the way to restore our Constitution to its rightful place. As Peacock explains, "Both the Constitution and the political science of *The Federalist* have been perennially attacked over America's 220-year history." The principles of our Founders "have come under assault from Anti-Federalists, Calhounites, social Darwinists, pragmatists, Progressives, postmodernists, deconstructionists, multiculturalists, transnationalists, and more. Yet the Constitution endures."

But it will continue to endure only if our leaders defend the principles of our Founders by consulting them in the midst of present troubles. And there is no better place to begin than *The Federalist Papers*.

Joseph Postell

Assistant Director, B. Kenneth Simon Center for American Studies,

The Heritage Foundation

INTRODUCTION

THE RELEVANCE OF *THE FEDERALIST*

Thomas Jefferson famously referred to *The Federalist* as "the best commentary on the principles of government, which ever was written."[1] Clinton Rossiter has claimed that *The Federalist* stands in third place among the greatest writings in American history, behind only the Declaration of Independence and the Constitution.[2] We might agree with this assessment, but we might also add an important qualification: Of these three documents in the pantheon of American political writings, *The Federalist* is least studied and least understood.

A case can certainly be made that the Declaration and the Constitution themselves are not studied very closely in American high schools, universities, or law schools; but in the case of *The Federalist*, the deficiency is even more stark. This is unfortunate since *The Federalist* can teach us more about the theory and practice of the Constitution than any other extant work. This book aims to reveal its basic teachings.

[1.] Andrew A. Lipscomb, ed., *The Writings of Thomas Jefferson* (Washington, D.C.: Thomas Jefferson Memorial Association, 1903), Vol. 7, p. 183.

[2.] Clinton Rossiter, "Introduction," in Alexander Hamilton, James Madison, and John Jay, *The Federalist Papers* (New York: New American Library, 1961), p. vii.

I

Over the past century, there has been open hostility among America's intellectuals to the natural rights philosophy on which the Declaration, the Constitution, and *The Federalist* are based. American social science, for instance, has carried the torch of German historicism and its American offspring, Pragmatism and Progressivism, since the turn of the 20th century.[3]

As Leo Strauss observed in 1953, according to modern social science, there are no such things as natural rights. All truth is relative, and, accordingly, all rights are positive rights, based one way or another on the preferences, prejudices, or historically contingent circumstances of the day. In the view of today's social science professoriate, the principles of natural right are mere "ideals" or mysticism or ideology, but they are certainly not true.[4]

This contempt for natural rights philosophy is dominant in American political science, where the teachings of the Declaration and America's Founders are frequently denigrated as affectations or idiosyncrasies of a bygone era—historical

---

3. Harvey Mansfield contrasts the "old rights" of classical liberalism and *The Federalist* with the "new," self-expressive rights of the New Deal and the 1960s. He says this of the latter: "As theory the new rights were born in Friedrich Nietzsche's doctrine of the creative self. How that doctrine came from Nietzsche's books of the late 1880s to American politics in the 1960s is a story that has not yet been fully told. One essential in the course of events is the historicism taken from German philosophy that was decisive in American pragmatism, for the pragmatists influenced the progressives and the progressives were predecessors of the New Deal." Harvey C. Mansfield, Jr., "Responsibility Versus Self-Expression," in *Old Rights and New*, ed. Robert A. Licht (Washington, D.C.: AEI Press, 1993), pp. 96, 103.

4. Leo Strauss, *Natural Right and History* (Chicago: University of Chicago Press, 1953), pp. 1–8 and 35–80. See also Harry V. Jaffa, *A New Birth of Freedom: Abraham Lincoln and the Coming of the Civil War* (Lanham, Md.: Rowman & Littlefield, 2000), esp. Ch. 2, "The Declaration of Independence, the Gettysburg Address, and the Historians," pp. 73–152.

anachronisms that, along with the Founders' Constitution, need to be eclipsed if a more rational, progressive, and egalitarian state capable of addressing today's technological and social problems is to flourish.

As one study of American political science has concluded: "Rejection of the Declaration of Independence, of its teachings, and of its applicability to our own times, was a necessary part of the foundation of a new American political science."[5] Rejection of the Founders' Constitution, and especially the political science of *The Federalist*, has been critical to both the establishment and the subsequent growth of the modern programmatic liberal state.

Since government has continually expanded into areas previously considered private for the past several generations, and as more people are becoming concerned about constitutional checks on government power, now would seem the perfect occasion to revisit the Founders' understanding of the Constitution and its relevant political science. And what better way to do that than by revisiting the most comprehensive guide to the Constitution and the Founders' political science: the essays on the Constitution that make up *The Federalist*.

The Federalist shares an exalted status with the Declaration and the Constitution because, better than any other writing in American political thought, it revealed the connection between these two foundational documents of American politics. Specifically, *The Federalist* demonstrated how the Constitution was an extension of the principles of the Declaration—especially the principles of liberty and equality—while at the same time illustrating how these principles had to be reconciled in a new constitutional instrument.

---

5. Dennis J. Mahoney, *Politics and Progress: The Emergence of American Political Science* (Lanham, Md.: Lexington Books, 2004), p. 75.

The Articles of Confederation failed to protect individual rights or promote the public good. In *Federalist* 40, Publius uses the Declaration to dispatch the Articles in favor of the Constitution. Claiming that "forms ought to give way to substance," he appeals directly to the Declaration for that "transcendent and precious right of the people to 'abolish or alter their governments as to them shall seem most likely to effect their safety and happiness.'" (*40:249*)[6]

Publius's meaning is clear: The Constitution is predicated upon the transcendent rights of the Declaration. Accordingly, Publius's task in *The Federalist* was to demonstrate the inherent *constitutionalism* of the new Constitution, its coherence as a political and republican document. The Constitution makes up a rational whole that will provide "a republican remedy for the diseases most incident to republican government" (*10:79*), and it is Publius's task to show how this whole fits together from architectonic principles to particular details.[7]

THE FEDERALIST AND THE RATIFICATION DEBATE

This guide to *The Federalist* is just that: a guide.[8] It is by no means comprehensive in its analysis, but in the pages that follow I hope to outline at least some of the basic teachings and central tenets of Publius's political philosophy and derivative political science. Publius is the pseudonym the authors of *The Federalist*—Alexander Hamilton, James Madison, and John Jay—attached to the end of each of their 85 papers making up

---

6. *Federalist* 40, in Alexander Hamilton, James Madison, and John Jay, *The Federalist Papers*, ed. Clinton Rossiter, intro. and notes Charles Kesler (New York: Signet Classic, 2003), p. 249. Essays in *The Federalist* are cited in this monograph by essay number (in *italics*) and page.

7. See also Kesler, "Introduction to *The Federalist Papers*," in Hamilton, Madison, and Jay, *The Federalist Papers*, p. viii.

the work. As was frequently the practice of the day, Hamilton, Madison, and Jay sought to remain anonymous as *The Federalist*'s authors.

Students of Plutarch's *Lives* are aware that Publius was short for Publius Valerius Publicola, the eloquent and noble Roman citizen who saved Roman republicanism.[9] Using the name "Publius," the authors of *The Federalist* apparently meant to suggest that their work—or their work in conjunction with the Constitution—was necessary to save American republicanism. They certainly implied that *The Federalist* was friendly to republicanism and (as their title made clear) to federalism. Use of a single pseudonym further suggested that *The Federalist* possessed a uniformity of intent: that *The Federalist* was to be read as the work of one mind, not three, and was coherent throughout. This monograph preserves that intention by attributing

---

8. The historical summary in the next six paragraphs draws from multiple sources, including Michael I. Meyerson, *Liberty's Blueprint: How Madison and Hamilton Wrote the Federalist Papers, Defined the Constitution, and Made Democracy Safe for the World* (New York: Basic Books, 2008); Willard Sterne Randall, *Alexander Hamilton: A Life* (New York: Perennial, 2004); Peter McNamara, *Political Economy and Statesmanship: Smith, Hamilton, and the Foundation of the Commercial Republic* (DeKalb, Ill.: Northern Illinois University Press, 1998); Lance Banning, *The Sacred Fire of Liberty: James Madison and the Founding of the Federal Republic* (Ithaca, N.Y.: Cornell University Press, 1995); Robert Scigliano, "Editor's Introduction," in Alexander Hamilton, John Jay, and James Madison, *The Federalist: A Commentary on the Constitution of the United States*, ed. and intro. Robert Scilgiano (New York: Modern Library, 2000); Kesler, "Introduction to The Federalist Papers," and Rossiter, "Introduction," in Hamilton, Madison, and Jay, *The Federalist Papers*.

9. Plutarch contrasts the life of Publius with the life of Solon. See Plutarch, *The Lives of the Noble Grecians and Romans*, Dryden trans., ed. and rev. Arthur Hugh Clough (New York: Modern Library, 1992), Vol. I, pp. 106–146.

each *Federalist* number to the work of Publius alone and not to any of the individual authors.

The Constitutional Convention took place in Philadelphia from May 25, 1787, to September 17, 1787. When the delegates left Philadelphia on September 17, it was evident that ratification of the new Constitution was not inevitable. It was unclear and even appeared unlikely that enough states would ratify the document.

Under Article VII, nine of the 13 states would have to ratify the Constitution before it could become the established law of the land. It was Hamilton's opinion that if the states failed to ratify the Constitution, America would disintegrate into a disparate archipelago of petty, jealous confederacies that would inevitably end up at war, and liberty in America would be lost.[10] With the stakes this high, Hamilton took it upon himself to provide a comprehensive, systematic response to those who criticized the Constitution or otherwise might jeopardize its ratification: primarily the Anti-Federalists but also other critics and fence-sitters whose failure to endorse the Constitution might entail its demise. Although the audience for *The Federalist* was initially to be New Yorkers, the papers published in the work eventually would be read outside the state as well.

As the architect of *The Federalist*, Hamilton planned in September 1787 to produce 20–25 papers in defense of the Constitution that would be published in newspapers in New York. However, by the time *The Federalist* began publication on October 27, it had become evident that a more ambitious project would be necessary.

---

10. See McNamara, *Political Economy and Statesmanship*, p. 109, and Scigliano, "Editor's Introduction," p. vii.

Ultimately, *The Federalist* would comprise 85 papers covering six general topics. The essays were published serially in New York and then elsewhere. At the height of their production, three or four new essays appeared each week.[11] Hamilton had arranged to have the collection of essays published in book form, and they were eventually published in two volumes. The first, published in March 1788, contained *Federalists* 1–36; the second, published in May 1788, appeared before the final eight essays had been published in the popular press.

Volume I of *The Federalist* was devoted to union and the necessity for more energetic government. Volume II was devoted to the Constitution and its conformity "to the true principles of republican government." (1:4) These subjects comported with the outline of *The Federalist* that Publius provided toward the end of *Federalist* 1.

Listed below (in italicized print) are the headings that Publius provided, summarizing the six topics with which *The Federalist* would deal. Listed in brackets next to those headings are *The Federalist* numbers that addressed those topics in the work's respective volumes. Following the fourth heading, I have also included subheadings, since *Federalists* 37–83 dealt with a host of issues concerning the general form of the Constitution and its structure.

As headings five and six make clear, the last two topics Publius intended to address were covered in a single *Federalist* number: *Federalist* 85. These headings did not need any further elaboration because they had "been so fully anticipated and exhausted in the progress of the work." (85:488–489) Accordingly, they were treated only briefly in *Federalist* 85.

---

11. See Kesler, "Introduction to *The Federalist Papers*," p. xi.

SUMMARY OF *THE FEDERALIST*

VOLUME I
[NOS. 1–36]

1. *The utility of the UNION to your political prosperity* [Nos. 1–14].

2. *The insufficiency of the present Confederation to preserve that Union* [Nos. 15–22].

3. *The necessity of a government at least equally energetic with the one proposed, to the attainment of this object* [Nos. 23–36].

VOLUME II
[NOS. 37–85]

4. *The conformity of the proposed Constitution to the true principles of republican government* [Nos. 37–84].

Nos. 37–40 General form of the Constitution—its republican and federal/national character.

Nos. 41–46 Sum or quantity of power vested in the government.

Nos. 47–51 Separation of powers.

Nos. 52–58 House of Representatives.

Nos. 59–61 Congressional regulation of elections.

Nos. 62–66 Senate.

Nos. 67–77 Executive.

Nos. 78–83 Judiciary.

No. 84 Responses to miscellaneous objections.

5. *Its analogy to your own State constitution* [No. 85].

6. *The additional security which its adoption will afford to the preservation of that species of government, to liberty, and to property* [No. 85].

In addition to himself, Hamilton enlisted the help of John Jay and, later, James Madison in writing the book. Although there is dispute over the authorship of certain *Federalist* numbers, Clinton Rossiter attributed 51 numbers to Hamilton, 26 to Madison, five to Jay, and three to Madison and Hamilton jointly.[12]

THE AUTHORS OF *THE FEDERALIST*

John Jay (1745–1829) was a New York lawyer of national stature and the oldest of the authors of *The Federalist*. He was 41 when he authored the few numbers he contributed to the work. He achieved prominence as one of the drafters of New York's 1777 constitution, president of the Continental Congress, chief justice of New York, principal negotiator of the Treaty of Paris (along with John Adams and Benjamin Franklin), and secretary of foreign affairs under the Confederation. Jay later served as the first Chief Justice of the United States Supreme Court, although he held this post for only six years before becoming governor of New York.

Unlike Hamilton and Madison, Jay did not attend the Constitutional Convention, because New York's Governor George Clinton had blocked his nomination to it. Nevertheless, Hamilton viewed Jay as one of the most astute political and legal minds of his day and conscripted him early to help co-author *The Federalist*. The principal reason Jay contributed as little as he did to the work was likely that after writing *Federalists* 2–5, he contracted rheumatoid arthritis and was unable to write again until many months later. His only other contribution to *The Federalist* was *Federalist* 64.

James Madison (1751–1836) has been heralded as the "father" of the Constitution, leading one of his biographers to

---

12. Rossiter, "Introduction," p. xi.

suggest that to misunderstand Madison's conduct and ideas is to misunderstand the Founding itself.[13] Madison attended the entirety of the Constitutional Convention and was influential in virtually every part of its deliberations. The notes he took in Philadelphia remain the only comprehensive written account of the discussions and debates that took place; the proceedings of the Convention were held in secret, and it was not until after his death in 1836 that Madison's notes from the Convention were published.[14]

Madison came from a wealthy Virginia family, was classically educated, and graduated from Princeton (then the College of New Jersey) in a mere two years. His extensive education and intimate familiarity with both ancient and modern political thought would serve him well both at the Federal Convention and in his work on *The Federalist.*

Madison met Hamilton in 1782 when both were members of the Continental Congress. Although the two were not close friends until their collaboration on *The Federalist,* they admired one another and agreed on the need for a new Constitution.

Alexander Hamilton (1755–1804) came from much more inauspicious beginnings than Madison. Born financially destitute on the British island of Nevis in the Caribbean, after emigrating to America in 1772 and locating in New York, Hamilton so distinguished himself as an artillery captain and

---

13. Banning, *The Sacred Fire of Liberty,* p. 2.
14. The editor of the most thorough collection of records from Philadelphia has written that "Madison's notes of the Debates have remained the standard authority for the proceedings of the Convention." Max Farrand, "Introduction," in Max Farrand, ed., *The Records of the Federal Convention* (New Haven, Conn.: Yale University Press, 1911), Vol. I, p. xvi.

soldier early in the Revolutionary War that George Washington made him his aide-de-camp and closest adviser.

Hamilton, whom many in New York's political elite recognized as a prodigy, not only excelled academically at King's College (now Columbia University), but wrote some of the most illuminating revolutionary writings while still in his twenties—writings that anticipated many of the arguments he would make in *The Federalist*. When the war ended, Hamilton practiced law full-time and later entered the Congress of the Confederation, where he would eventually become the principal draftsman of the resolution authorizing the Federal Convention.

The Federalist, like the Constitution, combines elements of the classical liberalism of the likes of John Locke, Adam Smith, David Hume, and Montesquieu with the republican tradition dating back to Periclean Athens and ancient Rome and as modified by more modern writers, including Publius. The Constitutional Convention, according to one popular account, was a "miracle" that brought together some of the best minds of early America and perhaps in the history of the West.[15]

Although *The Federalist* has been cited for over two centuries as the definitive historical authority on the Constitution by politicians, jurists, and constitutional commentators, it is its significance as a work of political and constitutional theory that has been least appreciated. That and its ongoing relevance to contemporary politics will be our focus below.

Note: Some of the material in this monograph appeared in Anthony A. Peacock, *Deconstructing the Republic: Voting Rights, the Supreme Court, and the Founders' Republicanism Reconsidered* (Washing-

---

[15]. See Catherine Drinker Bowen, *Miracle at Philadelphia: The Story of the Constitutional Convention May–September 1787* (Boston: Little, Brown, 1966).

ton, D.C.: AEI Press, 2008), and is reprinted here with the permission of the American Enterprise Institute for Public Policy Research, Washington, D.C.

Chapter 1

CONSTITUTIONAL GOVERNMENT, HUMAN NATURE, AND AMERICAN GREATNESS

Since *The Federalist* defends the establishment of government under the new Constitution, we might begin by asking what, precisely, Publius understands by "constitutional" government.

In simple terms, it is limited government: government limited to the powers enumerated in the Constitution and established by the consent of those governed. As noted above, Article VII of the Constitution required ratification by nine states for establishment of the Constitution. The Constitution was a social compact that required the consent of the people. As *Federalist* 22 affirmed, such consent was the "pure, original fountain of all legitimate authority" from which the "streams of national power ought to flow." (22:148) Like the Declaration of Independence, which established the natural equality of all, Publius asserts that all just powers derive from the consent of the governed.

THE FEDERALIST, HUMAN NATURE, AND LIMITED CONSTITUTIONAL GOVERNMENT

But if the natural equality of all is what the laws of nature dictate, those same laws reveal that human nature is less than perfect. As we will see, Publius argues that the Constitution can elevate human character,[16] but his political anthropology is otherwise based on a fixed and sober estimation of human nature. A few examples might illustrate the point.

Early in *The Federalist*, Publius warns that it is necessary for America to inoculate against giving foreign powers not only just causes of war against the United States, but also unjust or pretended causes of war, because it "is too true, however dis-

---

16. Commenting on the contrast between ancient and modern political philosophy, the latter including the "new science of politics" of the American Founders, Martin Diamond remarks: "The hallmark of the traditional ethics–politics relationship had been those harsh and comprehensive laws by means of which the ancient philosophers had sought to 'high-tone' human character. But now, because character formation was no longer the direct end of politics, the new science of politics could dispense with those laws and, for the achievement of its lowered ends, could rely largely instead upon shrewd institutional arrangements of the powerful human passions and interests. Not to instruct and to transcend these passions and interests, but rather to channel and to use them became the hallmark of modern politics." Martin Diamond, *As Far as Republican Principles Will Admit*, ed. William A. Schambra (Washington, D.C.: AEI Press, 1992), pp. 344–345. As I indicate below, Diamond's assessment of modern politics, and the Founders' constitutionalism in particular, as "solid but low" is fundamentally flawed, but his assumption is a common one among commentators on the political thinking of the American Founding. For a good discussion of how Alexander Hamilton understood the Constitution and how American commercial republicanism would cultivate American citizen virtue, see McNamara, *Political Economy and Statesmanship*, esp. p. 142, and Michael D. Chan, *Aristotle and Hamilton: On Commerce and Statesmanship* (Columbia: University of Missouri Press, 2006), esp. pp. 183–184.

graceful it may be to human nature, that nations in general will make war whenever they have a prospect of getting any thing by it." (4:40) Later, Publius proclaims "that men are ambitious, vindictive, and rapacious" (6:48) and that history has demonstrated "that momentary passions, and immediate interests, have a more active and imperious control over human conduct than general or remote considerations of policy, utility, or justice." (6:51)

In a famous passage from *Federalist* 51, Publius asks: "what is government itself but the greatest of all reflections on human nature? If men were angels, no government would be necessary. If angels were to govern men, neither external nor internal controls on government would be necessary." (51:319) In other words, both government and the governed have to be controlled. This is a fact of nature for which any form of government preservative of liberty will have to account.

The best way to control the federal government is to limit its powers. Contrary to the programmatic liberal state of potentially unlimited powers that today's federal government has become, Publius emphasized that the federal government of the Constitution would be a government of enumerated and limited powers. The "great and aggregate interests" would be "referred to the national" government, whereas "the local and particular" interests would be referred "to the State legislatures." (10:77-8) With this natural division between state and federal powers constraining the national government, Publius outlined the four "principal purposes" of the new constitutional union:

1. "[T]he common defense of the members";

2. "[T]he preservation of the public peace, as well against internal convulsions as external attacks";

3. "[T]he regulation of commerce with other nations and between the States"; and

4. "[T]he superintendence of [America's] intercourse, political and commercial, with foreign countries." $(23:149)^{17}$

The powers enumerated in the first two articles of the Constitution, which define congressional and executive powers, comported with these broad outlines of limited federal power.

Publius affirms that men are both self-interested and ambitious. Their opinions are driven more by passion and self-love than they are by reason. This connection between self-love and one's opinions is what leads so readily to faction, that most "dangerous vice" of popular governments that "a well constructed Union" must "break and control." The difficulty is that the "latent causes of faction are...sown in the nature of man." The "zeal for different opinions concerning religion, concerning government, and many other points" makes men "much more disposed to vex and oppress each other than to co-operate for their common good." In fact, "[s]o strong is this propensity of mankind to fall into mutual animosities that where no substantial occasion presents itself the most frivolous and fanciful distinctions have been sufficient to kindle their unfriendly passions and excite their most violent conflicts."

Publius qualifies that "the most common and durable source of factions has been the various and unequal distribution of property" and that "[t]hose who hold and those who are without property have ever formed distinct interests in society," but it is evident from his emphasis that the most violent conflicts originate in passion, not interest. (*10*:71-4)

---

17. See also *Federalist* 17:114.

This distinction is critical because it suggests that the Constitution was intended to mitigate two basic forms of political conflict: conflict that originates in human *passion*, especially collective passion such as pride, hatred, and vanity,[18] and conflict that originates in *interests*, specifically those related to property. Faction is famously defined in *Federalist* 10 in these dichotomous terms, being understood as "a number of citi-

---

[18.] See *Federalist* 15:106: "Why has government been instituted at all? Because the passions of men will not conform to the dictates of reason and justice without constraint. Has it been found that bodies of men act with more rectitude or greater disinterestedness than individuals? The contrary of this has been inferred by all accurate observers of the conduct of mankind; and the inference is founded upon obvious reasons. Regard to reputation has a less active influence when the infamy of a bad action is to be divided among a number than when it is to fall singly upon one. A spirit of faction, which is apt to mingle its poison in the deliberations of all bodies of men, will often hurry the persons of whom they are composed into improprieties and excesses for which they would blush in a private capacity." See also Hans A. Linde, "When Initiative Lawmaking Is Not 'Republican Government': The Campaign Against Homosexuality," *Oregon Law Review*, Vol. 72 (1993), pp. 19, 32: "Republican government must be responsive to the people, but what both history and recent experience in the states led the framers to fear was unbridled 'interest' and 'passion.' These were well-known terms in Enlightenment political theory, and nothing since has made them obscure. By the end of the seventeenth century, 'interest' had a specifically economic meaning. Individual 'passion' included noneconomic motives like pride and ambition. But only collective passion endangered a system built on collective action. Hume's *Treatise on Human Nature* in 1740 distinguished between the passion of interest, or 'love of gain,' which is 'perpetual' and 'universal,' from intermittent passions of envy and revenge directed against other persons. Collective passions, now as then, unite groups by national, racial, ethnic, or tribal loyalties and inherited hatreds, or by a shared sense of religious truth or moral outrage, that divide 'us' from 'them' without any personal target.... To the federalists, collective 'passion' was the antithesis of 'reason.'"

zens, whether amounting to a majority or minority of the whole, who are united and actuated by some common impulse of passion, or of interest, adverse to the rights of other citizens, or to the permanent and aggregate interests of the community." (*10*:72)

As Publius's definition here suggests, the two principal ends that the Constitution was to secure were the public good and private or individual rights. Faction, which was endemic to the human condition, endangered both of these ends. The Constitution sought to mitigate the effects of faction by, on the one hand, making it difficult for a majority faction to infringe individual rights or to undermine the public good and, on the other hand, channeling faction into the less volatile forms of human conflict anchored in disputes over interests or property.

History had amply demonstrated to America's Founders that the nadir of European politics had been those episodes of violent religious warfare in which the passions of pride and hatred had been unleashed in the name of religious and ethnic chauvinism.[19] As a student of classical liberalism, Publius knew that collective passion had precipitated the most bloody and explosive political conflicts in European history, conflicts ignited (as Madison suggested in *Federalist* 10) by the most friv-

---

[19.] Madison's speech at the Constitutional Convention on June 6, 1787—the precursor to his argument in *Federalist* 10—inveighed that "Religion itself may become a motive to persecution & oppression" and that "We have seen the mere distinction of colour made in the most enlightened period of time, a ground of the most oppressive dominion ever exercised by man over man." Farrand, *The Records of the Federal Convention of 1787*, Vol. I, p. 135. Classifying citizens on the basis of religion and race was illiberal and could precipitate the most violent forms of political conflict. Article VI of the Constitution made clear that "no religious Test shall ever be required as a Qualification to any Office or public Trust under the United States."

olous of causes. Classical liberals like Hobbes, Locke, Montesquieu, and Hume had all demonstrated that as much as men
were divided naturally by their passions, they could be united
artificially by their interests.[20]

This is not to say, of course, that economic interests do
not result in contention or even hostilities. To the contrary,
Federalists 6 and 7 are an exposé of the violence that can result
from dueling commercial interests, both domestically and in
matters of foreign affairs.[21] But in *Federalists* 9–14, Publius
shows how commerce, at least as directed and moderated by
the new Constitution, can also promote comity, union, and
American greatness. In fact, the most distinct elements of the
improved "science of politics" that Publius introduces in *Federalist* 9 are not the four specific improvements to that science
that we learn in any basic American government class: separation of powers, legislative checks and balances, an independent

---

20. See Hiram Caton, *The Politics of Progress: The Origins and Development of the
Commercial Republic, 1600–1835* (Gainesville: University of Florida
Press, 1988), p. 470. For a good survey of the centuries-old philosophical treatment of the distinction between interest and passion in
classical liberal thought, see Albert O. Hirschman, *The Passions and the
Interests: Political Arguments for Capitalism Before Its Triumph* (Princeton, N.J.:
Princeton University Press, 1997). As Hirschman remarks: "Ever
since the end of the Middle Ages, and particularly as a result of the
increasing frequency of war and civil war in the seventeenth and eigh-
teenth centuries, the search was on for a behavioral equivalent for the
religious precept, for new rules of conduct and devices that would
impose much needed discipline and constraints on both rulers and
ruled, and the expansion of commerce and industry was thought to
hold much promise in this regard." Hirschman, *The Passions and the Interests*, p. 129.

21. "Has commerce hitherto done any thing more than change the objects
of war?" Publius queried in *Federalist* 6. "Is not the love of wealth as
domineering and enterprising a passion as that of power or glory?"
Federalist 6:51. Commerce and the love of wealth could certainly facilitate conflict, as the historical examples cited by Publius illustrated.

judiciary, and representation of the people. Rather, the most novel and important contribution to political science that the Constitution will make is "the ENLARGEMENT of the ORBIT," the extended sphere of territory over which the new federal republic will preside. (9:67)

THE EXTENDED REPUBLIC

Publius's defense of the Constitution was a theoretical defense of a new concept of republicanism spread over a large territory. His constitutionalism rejected two long-standing assumptions of classical and modern political thought: *first*, that only in direct democracies or small republics could stability and virtue be promoted and, *second*, that commerce was debasing and that its promotion spurred inequality, avarice, selfishness, vanity, and undue consumption and pursuit of luxury, as Jean-Jacques Rousseau, perhaps the most famous critic of 18th century commercial society, had maintained.[22]

On the first issue, the problem with direct democracies and small republics was that they were prone to majority tyranny since a common passion or interest will invariably overtake a majority of those who make political decisions. State governments under the Articles of Confederation had largely exemplified this pathology. Large republics, by contrast, and particularly the republic proposed by the Constitution, could undermine majority tyranny or faction both institutionally and socially.

Institutionally, constitutional provisions such as the separation of powers, checks and balances, the federal structure of government, and the variety of terms and methods of election

---

[22.] See, for instance, Jean-Jacques Rousseau, *Discours sur les sciences et les arts* and *Discours sur l'origine, et les fondemens de l'inégalité parmi les hommes*, in *Oeuvres complètes* (Paris: Gallimard, 1964), Vol. III, pp. 1 and 109.

for Members of Congress and the President could check factions *after* they had formed. Such factions, however, needed to be undermined *before* they could form at the level of society as well.[23] The enlarged republic created by the Constitution would directly assist this object. As Publius famously put it:

> Extend the sphere, and you take in a greater variety of parties and interests; you make it less probable that a majority of the whole will have a common motive to invade the rights of other citizens; or if such a common motive exists, it will be more difficult for all who feel it to discover their own strength and to act in unison with each other." (*10*:78)[24]

The extended sphere would complement the Constitution's *institutional* checks on faction by multiplying the economic, social, and religious interests that made up society to such an extent that they would rarely, if ever, be able to coalesce into collective or "class" interests that might oppress a minority.

---

[23] As Publius remarked: "It is of great importance in a republic not only to guard the society against the oppression of its rulers, but to guard one part of the society against the injustice of the other part." *Federalist* 51:320. See also Diamond, *As Far as Republican Principles Will Admit*, pp. 53–57.

[24] See also *Federalist* 51:322: "In the extended republic of the United States, and among the great variety of interests, parties, and sects which it embraces, a coalition of a majority of the whole society could seldom take place upon any other principles than those of justice and the general good."

THE DIFFERENCE BETWEEN
REPUBLICANISM AND DEMOCRACY

The critical difference between republican and democratic government (by which Publius meant direct democracy) was that republican government could incorporate a "greater number of citizens and extent of territory" than democracies could. Importantly, Publius emphasized that it was "*this* circumstance *principally* which render[ed] factious combinations less to be dreaded in the former than in the latter." (10:78; emphasis added) In other words, as important as institutional or governmental checks on faction were, it was the *non-institutional* or societal checks afforded by the Constitution's extended republic that were most crucial.

The implication of Publius's argument, as political scientist Martin Diamond has observed, was that not just any large republic would do for purposes of the Constitution's prescriptions against faction. Only a large *commercial* republic could solve the problem of faction since it was only in such a republic that property interests could be sufficiently differentiated that the class conflict that had been the bane of republics since time immemorial could be eviscerated.

The "first object of government," Publius stressed, is to protect the "the faculties of men, from which the rights of property originate." However:

> From the protection of different and unequal faculties of acquiring property, the possession of different *degrees* and *kinds* of property immediately results; and from the influence of these on the sentiments and views of the respective proprietors ensues a division of the society into different interests and parties.... Those who hold and those who are without property have ever formed

distinct interests in society. (*10*:73-4; emphasis added)

By replacing divisions over *degrees or amounts* of property with divisions over *kinds* of property, the ages-old conflict between rich and poor could largely be overcome. Just as the Constitution would subordinate racial and religious classifications to economic classifications, so also would the extended sphere reduce those economic classifications themselves from the historically fatal class struggles that plagued pre-modern republics to the safe, even salutary, struggles between ever more differentiated kinds of propertied interests that would flourish under the Constitution.[25]

It is important to note that although Publius saw the extended sphere as a remedy for the diseases of faction, it was not a panacea. Publius was not an economic determinist who, in the tradition of modern behavioral social science, looked at men as simple stimulus-response mechanisms bent on maximizing their self-interest.[26] For one thing, human interests do not emerge *ex nihilo*. They have to be created and shaped.

---

25. Diamond, *As Far as Republican Principles Will Admit*, pp. 53–57, 351–352, and 391. For a critique of Diamond's interpretation of *The Federalist* and, specifically, Madison's thought concerning "commercial republicanism," see Banning, *The Sacred Fire of Liberty*, pp. 205–212. Banning rejects that Madison ever accepted Hamilton's understanding of "commercial republicanism" and points out that Madison himself never referred "to the United States as a 'commercial society' or a 'commercial republic,' as Hamilton does in *Federalist* no. 6." *Ibid.*, p. 212. Banning's interpretation is difficult to square with *Federalist* 10 and 51, in addition to other writings and speeches of Madison's. Moreover, the identity established between Hamilton's and Madison's writings in *The Federalist*, evidenced by the use of a single pseudonym, "Publius," suggests, as I indicated earlier, that Hamilton's and Madison's thought throughout *The Federalist* was intended to make up a single, coherent whole.

Moreover, men often do not know what their true interests are, and if they do, they are frequently blinded to them by their immediate inclinations and passions.

Individual life, like politics, is typically infected by enthusiasm; thus, to assume that men are going to act like rational calculators is to systematize politics in a way that Publius rejected as the affectation of "[t]heoretic politicians." (*10*:76)[27] Men do not *behave* predictably so much as *act* freely.[28] Accordingly, the extended sphere, as effective as it might be as a control on the effects of faction, was not foolproof.

Nor did Publius advocate the protection of property rights and development of commerce as mere expedients, the best remedies for the problem of faction. In *Federalist* 10, Publius denounced the "rage for paper money, for an abolition of debts, for an equal division of property" as "improper or wicked project[s]." (*10*:79) Redistribution of wealth—taking from Peter to give to Paul—was immoral. Such projects undercut the imperative of responsible self-governance, the

---

26. For the consummate statement on *The Federalist*, and particularly *Federalist* 10, as promoting a doctrine of economic determinism, see Charles A. Beard, *An Economic Interpretation of the Constitution of the United States*, intro. Forrest McDonald (New York: Free Press, 1986). Beard writes of *The Federalist*: "This wonderful piece of argumentation by Hamilton, Madison, and Jay is in fact the finest study in the economic interpretation of politics which exists in any language; and whoever would understand the Constitution as an economic document need hardly go beyond it." *Ibid.*, p. 153. For a critique of the limitations of Beard's analysis, see Charles R. Kesler, "*Federalist* 10 and American Republicanism," in *Saving the Revolution: The Federalist Papers and the American Founding*, ed. Charles R. Kesler (New York: Free Press, 1987), p. 13 and esp. pp. 16–19.

27. See also McNamara, *Political Economy and Statesmanship*, pp. 97–98.

28. See Rainer Knopff, *Human Rights and Social Technology: The New War on Discrimination* (Ottawa: Carleton University Press, 1990), p. 205.

value of work, and those most fundamental rights of property. The protection of property and promotion of commerce were not only critical for the amelioration of faction, in other words, but also part of the Constitution's moral order, its cultivation of high politics and protection of political and moral principle.

The concept of human nature developed in *The Federalist* was, then, composed of both low and high elements. Human nature may be largely fixed, but it is also capable of guidance and sublimation. The protection of property and promotion of commerce were critical to this latter task, although they were obviously not sufficient for the full cultivation of human faculties and virtues. Commercial development was the necessary precondition for the generation of wealth, which made civilization itself possible.[29] It promoted equality of opportunity and gave all, including the poor, the chance to rise up socially and economically. It facilitated industry and induced everyone to work and avoid sloth.[30]

Property interests were rational interests not only because they were necessary to the support of life and liberty, but also because, being tangible, they directed men's attention to con-

---

[29.] As Publius remarked: "A landed interest, a manufacturing interest, a mercantile interest, a moneyed interest, with many lesser interests, grow up *of necessity in civilized* nations." *Federalist* 10:74; emphasis added.

[30.] On these themes, see Anthony A. Peacock, "The Voting Rights Act and the Politics of Multiculturalism: The Challenge to Commercial Republicanism at Century's Turn," in *Courts and the Culture Wars*, ed. Bradley C. S. Watson (Lanham, Md.: Lexington Books, 2002), pp. 167, 185–186; Drew R. McCoy, *The Elusive Republic: Political Economy in Jeffersonian America* (Chapel Hill: University of North Carolina Press, 1980); Karl-Friedrich Walling, *Republican Empire: Alexander Hamilton on War and Free Government* (Lawrence: University Press of Kansas, 1999); and Chan, *Aristotle and Hamilton.*

crete realities—specifically, those concrete realities that might be improved. As much as they could result in conflict, as *Federalists* 6 and 7 highlighted, they also directed men's attention to the longer-term view of political order and thus held out the promise of reconciliation and the promotion of good government, as *Federalists* 9–14 made clear.[31] When enumerating those "three descriptions of men" who would be chosen to represent the people in Congress, it was no accident that *The Federalist* outlined predominantly economic categories: "landholders, merchants, and men of the learned professions." (35:212)

This is not to say, of course, that Americans were simply economic beings or that they would be defined solely or principally by commercial relations under the Constitution. To the contrary, the economic freedoms that the Constitution promoted would be equaled or surpassed by those political and other liberties that the Constitution promised to secure. Publius was as interested in accommodating man's *political* impulses as he was in accommodating man's *economic* impulses.[32]

Those political impulses, however, had their limit. The Constitution was based on principles of limited and responsi-

---

[31] See Caton, *The Politics of Progress*, p. 472; Hirschman, *The Passions and the Interests*, pp. 9–66. As Walter Berns has remarked, unlike other forms of faction, such as those based on religion, "property factions could be regulated (and accommodated) because, although divided from one another, they shared a common interest in economic growth, and to promote this growth would be the task of modern legislation. America's business would be (as Calvin Coolidge many years later said it was) business." Walter Berns, "Constitutionalism and Multiculturalism," in *Multiculturalism and American Democracy*, eds. Arthur M. Melzer, Jerry Weinberger, and M. Richard Zinman (Lawrence: University Press of Kansas, 1998), pp. 91, 96.

[32] See David F. Epstein, *The Political Theory of The Federalist* (Chicago: University of Chicago Press, 1984), p. 6.

ble government. Its commercial republicanism reduced the scope of the political in the pre-modern, pre-liberal sense primarily (although not solely) to issues of political economy—national defense, domestic order, foreign and interstate commerce—not only because this was prudent and the precondition for civic harmony, but also because constitutional principle and individual liberty required it.

THE CONSTITUTION'S ENDS: NOT "SOLID BUT LOW"

Ironically, many students of *The Federalist* have interpreted Publius's defense of the Constitution's limited government and commercial republicanism as an admission that the objects of American politics were "solid but low." The Founders' Constitution, Diamond proclaimed, focused on promoting security and comfortable well-being, effectively removing "from political life...what had for two thousand years been regarded as its chief function, namely, ethical character formation based on some elevated view of the 'advantageous or just.'"[33] Publius, however, would disagree with such a narrow interpretation of either the Constitution's ends or its relation to character formation.

First, despite the limited government objectives of the Constitution, Publius did not see the amelioration of faction, the promotion of wealth, or even the provision of security as the only ends—or even the highest ends—of the Constitution. As he declared in *Federalist* 51: "Justice is the end of government. It is the end of civil society. It ever has been and ever will be pursued until it be obtained, or until liberty be lost in the pursuit." (51:321) As the preamble to the Constitution makes

---

[33.] Diamond, *As Far as Republican Principles Will Admit,* pp. 355–356, 344, and 346.

clear, the Constitution was ordained to "establish Justice." Far from being aimed at the "solid but low," the American Constitution was guided by the highest goal that both ancient and modern political philosophy had to offer: the idea of justice.

Second, for Publius, constitutional reform was impossible without moral and civic reform. Publius lamented that the Articles of Confederation had reduced Americans to "almost the last stage of national humiliation. There [was] scarcely any thing that can wound the pride or degrade the character of an independent nation which [Americans did] not experience." (*15*:101) The federal government had to "be able to address itself immediately to the hopes and fears of individuals; and to attract to its support those passions which have the strongest influence upon the human heart." (*16*:111)

As well as any Founder, Publius understood the necessity of attaching those intangible elements of state power—men's passions—to the tangible instruments of state, particularly the Constitution's provisions for political and economic improvement and military expansion.[34] All were critical, in Publius's eye, to harnessing American pride or Americans' passionate sense of honor to the Constitution. Moreover, republican government, more than any other form of government, required citizen virtue since it was based on the principle of self-government. In *Federalist* 55, Publius observes:

> As there is a degree of depravity in mankind which requires a certain degree of circumspection and distrust, so there are other qualities in human nature which justify a certain portion of esteem and confidence. Republican government presupposes the existence of these qualities in a higher degree than any other form. Were the pic-

---

34. Walling, *Republican Empire*, pp. 43 and 70.

tures which have been drawn by the political jealousy of some among us faithful likenesses of the human character, the inference would be that there is not sufficient virtue among men for self-government; and that nothing less than the chains of despotism can restrain them from destroying and devouring one another. (55:343)

The Constitution not only requires civic virtue in the citizens at-large, but also presupposes it at a very high level of development. Republican government, Publius argues, "presupposes" those elevated "qualities" of human nature "in a higher degree than *any other form.*" Thus, contrary to the opinions of Diamond and others who believe that American republicanism is built upon "solid but low" foundations, Publius suggests the opposite: Republicanism, as the highest form of government predicated upon the principle of self-reliance, requires the highest virtue from its citizens. Without such virtue, republicanism will necessarily fail.

As we will see below, the precondition for the development of both American honor and the citizen virtue necessary to maintain republicanism is not merely the Constitution, but union.

Chapter 2

UNION AND CITIZENSHIP

*A*s the Constitution would give birth to a government of limited objects that would also be objects of common, never particular, concern, the precondition for this was union and its corollary of a uniform concept of citizenship. Although Americans until recently have assumed the existence of a firm political union, issues like illegal immigration, the application of international law to American domestic politics, the litany of group rights institutionalized under federal and state affirmative action programs since the 1970s, and the dominance of special-interest or clientele politics in national government have all worked to undermine both the notion of union and a common American citizenship.

THE NECESSITY OF UNION

The first half of *The Federalist* (*Federalists* 1–36) was a defense of the necessity of strong union, a union that in 1787 stood on the brink of dissolving. The Articles of Confederation had failed to constitute an effective concept of American nationhood or political union. Indeed, as we often learn in histories of the period, Americans in 1787 identified more with their states than they did with "America."

Given that the meaning of union in the 1780s was so opaque, the authors of *The Federalist* saw it as a principal task in their defense of the Constitution to clarify its significance. Accordingly, *Federalists* 2–14 dealt specifically with the question of "*[t]he utility of the UNION to your political prosperity.*" (*1*:30; emphasis in original) We might ask then: What exactly *was* the utility of the union to Americans' political prosperity as *The Federalist* understood this?

Publius's responses to this question were both practical and theoretical, and moved from the realm of basic military necessity to the realm of public-spiritedness and freedom. The most obvious practical end that the new constitutional union would promote was security: security from foreign danger, from that civil discord certain to arise between the several confederacies that would emerge absent federal union, security from despotism, and security from domestic faction. The proposed integration of manufacturing, agricultural, and other economic interests that Publius hoped might cultivate political comity and a sense of "Americanness" was also impossible without union: "A unity of commercial, as well as political, interests can only result from a unity of government." (*11*:85)

Cultivating a sense of American identity or patriotism— "making patriots"[35] as Walter Berns has put it—was a central task of *The Federalist*. The theoretical account of union was perhaps the most interesting aspect of its defense. The new constitutional union was a political necessity, but it was also ennobling. The union and the Constitution that would sustain it would be the means through which a newly conceived citizenship and accompanying public-spiritedness might be facilitated.[36]

This was one of the reasons why the notion of a political and commercial union was so critical. Critics of the Constitu-

---

[35]. Walter Berns, *Making Patriots* (Chicago: University of Chicago Press, 2001).

tion who wanted to reduce America to a confederate archipelago of predominantly agrarian republics with limited industry
overlooked what was perhaps most unique about American
character and held out so much promise for national greatness
and American pride. Political and commercial union would
provide not only tangible benefits, but also—and perhaps as
important—the intangible benefits of cultivating a love of
country and identification of constitutional union with political strength and fortitude.

Publius commended the "adventurous spirit" that distinguished "the commercial character of America" and that had
by 1787 "already excited uneasy sensations in several of the
maritime powers of Europe." (11:79) He invited Americans
"to aim at an ascendant in the system of American affairs," to
erect "one great American system," "to vindicate the honor"
not merely of America, but "of the human race." Americans,
he concluded, should "disdain to be the instruments of European greatness." (11:85-6) They should, in other words, pursue their own greatness: one more principled—because
anchored in consent—than the greatness pursued by the imperial powers of the day.

In the very first paragraph of *The Federalist*, Publius had
made a similar invocation. There he identified perpetuation of
"the existence of the UNION" with "the fate of an empire in
many respects the most interesting in the world." Failure to
ratify the Constitution would demonstrate that "societies of
men" are incapable "of establishing good government from
reflection and choice" but are rather "forever destined to

---

36. See, for instance, *Federalist* 41:255: "Every man who loves peace, every
man who loves his country, every man who loves liberty ought to have
it ever before his eyes that he may cherish in his heart a due attachment to the Union of America and be able to set a due value on the
means of preserving it."

depend for their political constitutions on accident and force." Rejecting the Constitution would be a misfortune not just for America, but for all "of mankind." (*I:27*)

THE AMERICAN EXPERIMENT AND THE FATE OF SELF-GOVERNMENT

Why was America so interesting, and why was ratification of the Constitution so important not merely for Americans, but for all of mankind?

Publius emphasized that ratification of the Constitution would contribute not only to Americans' "liberty" and "happiness," but also to their "dignity." (*1:30*) The reason seemed to be the connection between choice, honor, and political principle. As the Declaration of Independence made clear, republican government or government by consent was the only just form of government. However, if republicanism was to be vindicated as a form of political regime, it had to be shown that it could actually work.

As Publius pointed out in *Federalist* 9, those "petty republics of Greece and Italy" that were exemplars of pre-modern republicanism for so many of the Anti-Federalists perpetually vibrated "between the extremes of tyranny and anarchy." Their short-lived periods of political calm were "soon to be overwhelmed by the tempestuous waves of sedition and party rage." In addition, they were plagued by those "vices of government" that served to "pervert the direction and tarnish the luster of those bright talents and exalted endowments for which the favored soils that produced them have been so justly celebrated." The Platos, Aristotles, and Ciceros of Greek and Roman antiquity, in other words, had flourished not *because of* but *in spite of* the regimes of which they were a part.

America's new constitutional order would correct this pre-modern defect. It would avoid the vices of government by creating the conditions in which the talented and the highly endowed could flourish. But Publius immediately qualifies: The portraits sketched by the critics "of republican government were too just copies of the originals from which they were taken." (9:66–7)

Republicanism had a sorry history, and one did not have to look too far back in Europe's past to see this. It was up to Americans to vindicate the legacy of republicanism. This, however, would require choice and, more specifically (as *Federalist* I made clear), deliberative choice; choice by itself would not be good enough.

The post-Revolutionary decade had demonstrated this. The Articles of Confederation were freely chosen by the American people but had been a political and economic disaster. They illustrated the extent to which republican government was not synonymous with free government. Free government required not merely choosing, but choosing wisely, since only such choice could vindicate American honor and, by implication, the honor of mankind. Only by choosing good government—choosing the Constitution over the Articles of Confederation— could the American people demonstrate that men were capable of being governed by "reflection and choice" rather than by "accident and force."

PRINCIPLE OVER CULTURE

Another question raised about union was whether it was based solely on the principles of the Declaration or also on something cultural like a Judeo–Christian or Anglo–American heritage. In *Federalist* 2, Publius observes:

> Providence has been pleased to give this one connected country to one united people—a people descended from the same ancestors, speaking the

same language, professing the same religion, attached to the same principles of government, very similar in their manners and customs, and who, by their joint counsels, arms, and efforts, fighting side by side throughout a long and bloody war, have nobly established their general liberty and independence. (2:32)

The emphasis here is on Americans' being "attached to the same principles of government" and fighting a revolutionary war that "nobly established their general liberty and independence." The Revolutionary War was noble because it was just, and it was just because it was fought for political principles: for equal rights and equal recognition of universal natural rights.

Publius, however, adds something here. He suggests a "religious" or "cultural" unity thesis as the basis for American constitutionalism in addition to—or perhaps as a substitute for—a social compact theory of constitutional union.[37] Americans descend "from the same ancestors," speak "the same language," profess "the same religion." In *Federalist* 14, Publius argues that there is a "kindred blood which flows in the veins of American citizens, the mingled blood which they have shed in defense of their sacred rights." (14:99)

What does Publius mean by these remarks? Does unity depend on a common culture? It is certainly plausible that such a culture may be one reason—even a critical reason—for American union. A common English language and religious heritage, for instance, may unite Americans in a common cause

[37]. For a good commentary on this distinction, see Bradley C. S. Watson, "Creed & Culture in the American Founding," *The Intercollegiate Review*, Vol. 41, No. 2 (Fall 2006), p. 32, and James W. Ceaser, "How to Think About the Foundations of American Conservatism," Heritage Foundation *First Principles* No. 22, December 10, 2008, p. 1.

in a way that they would not be united with French or Spanish Catholics.

But Publius is quick to emphasize that Anglo–American or Judeo–Christian heritage is insufficient to unite Americans. In *Federalist* 5, for instance, he makes clear that, despite whatever common cultural heritage Americans may share, "it is far more probable that in America, as in Europe, neighboring nations, acting under the impulse of opposite interests and unfriendly passions, would frequently be found taking different sides." (5:47) Whatever blood ties Americans may share will be broken soon enough after disunion by their conflicting ambitions, interests, and passions. Neighbors who share borders tend to go to war no matter who they are and what affinities they share. Anyone who thinks that the United States divided into "partial confederacies" would not be riven by "frequent and violent contests with each other," Publius declares, "must be far gone in Utopian speculations." (6:48)

More important, the true glue that unites Americans is the revolutionary principles on which the Constitution is based; shared "political principles" and "sacred rights," not ethnoracial bloodlines or ties of religion, are the real basis of constitutional union. Recall Publius's declaration from *Federalist* 22 that the "fabric of American empire ought to rest on the solid basis of the CONSENT OF THE PEOPLE." (22:148) Americans may share a "kindred blood," but it is a "mingled blood" shed in defense of Americans' "sacred rights"—the rights of the Revolution that are both sublime and universal.[38]

As if to place an exclamation mark on this point, Publius concludes *Federalist* 14 by noting that it is "the glory of the people of America" not to have "suffered a blind veneration for antiquity, for custom, or for names" and to have relied instead on "their own good sense, the knowledge of their own situation, and the lessons of their own experience" to reject the traditional in favor of novelty, especially the novelty of the Revolution.

> [P]osterity will be indebted for the possession, and the world for the example, of the numerous innovations displayed on the American theatre in favor of private rights and public happiness.... Happily for America, happily we trust for the whole human race, [Americans] pursued a new and more noble course. They accomplished a revolution which has no parallel in the annals of human society. (*14*:99-100)

In other words, the traditional, cultural, and particular were rejected in favor of the principled and universal. The patriotism facilitated by the new constitutional union, then, would not be the irrational sort that originates in an ethnic, religious, or martial chauvinism of the type that had plagued pre-liberal regimes. Rather, American nationalism or citizenship would be anchored in the universally legitimate principles of liberty and consent, which made no distinctions between groups or individuals.

Publius further hoped that the new constitutional union would rear the "fabric of American empire" that might eventually compete commercially and militarily with the world

---

38. See also *Federalist* 39:236: "The first question that offers itself is whether the general form and aspect of the government [under the Constitution] be strictly republican. It is evident that no other form would be reconcilable with the genius of the people of America; with the fundamental principles of the Revolution; or with that honorable determination which animates every votary of freedom to rest all our political experiments on the capacity of mankind for self-government. If the plan of the convention, therefore, be found to depart from the republican character, its advocates must abandon it as no longer defensible."

empires of the day, those imperial powers of the 18th century that had extended modern commerce worldwide and had defined modern warfare, which was total and required virtually every sinew of the state to contribute to a nation's military wherewithal.[39] "A nation, despicable by its weakness," Publius declared, "forfeits even the privilege of being neutral." (11:82) Even the citizens of a weak state will despise it.

UNION, SECURITY, AND WORLD AFFAIRS

To preserve America's freedom to choose political options in domestic and foreign affairs required that America have the military wherewithal to survive in the modern world, but in 1787 America was surrounded on all sides by danger. Imperial Britain had settlements that stretched far into the American hinterland of the West and North, and imperial Spain had settlements that reached up to the British settlements, engulfing the American South. Despite an ocean that separated the United States from Europe, improvements in navigation had rendered distant nations neighbors. (24:157)

Those who insisted that militias would be adequate to America's national defense and who opposed a standing army under the Constitution did not understand the nature of modern warfare and its perils. "War, like most other things, is a science to be acquired and perfected by diligence, by perseverance, by time, and by practice." (25:162) America needed a navy and a professional army. It also needed development of the arts and sciences, especially the military sciences.

---

39. In *Federalist* 11, Publius anticipated: "There can be no doubt that the continuance of the Union under an efficient government would put it in our power, at a period not very distant, to create a navy which, if it could not vie with those of the great maritime powers, would at least be of respectable weight if thrown into the scale of either of two contending parties." *Federalist* 11:81.

In addition, America needed the constitutional means to provide for public finance, particularly public borrowing, that essential tool of modern political economy that had opened up such vast quantities of wealth for the conduct of modern war.[40] "In the modern system of war," even "nations the most wealthy are obliged to have recourse to large loans." (*30*:187) "The means of revenue...the arts of industry, and the science of finance," Publius concluded, "concurring with the habits of nations, have produced an entire revolution in the system of war." (*8*:63)

Only the new constitutional union could accommodate this revolution. By integrating commercial and military wherewithal, the new union would provide for greater security as well as the division of labor that would enhance productivity through specialization. Industriousness and ingenuity would also be promoted, and the opportunity to cultivate the kaleidoscope of natural talents that only an advanced commercial society could develop would flourish.[41]

Perhaps above all, the integration of military and commercial development might again promote union and American pride. To that "great national object, a NAVY," Publius argued, "union will contribute in various ways. Every institution will grow and flourish in proportion to the quantity and extent of the means concentered towards its formation and support"; but a navy "would embrace the resources of all," harmonizing interests by integrating the agricultural South with the industrial North in a single, dynamic commercial union. A federal navy and the political and economic integration that it would facilitate might have the intangible benefit of forging a

---

[40.] See *Federalist* 41:258: "The power of levying and borrowing money, being the sinew of that which is to be exerted in the national defense, is properly thrown into the same class with it." See also McNamara, *Political Economy and Statesmanship*, p. 110.

new American national identity born of effective, energetic, and even inspirational government:

> Under a vigorous national government, the natural strength and resources of the country, directed to a common interest, would baffle all the combinations of European jealousy to restrain [American] growth. This situation would even take away the motive to such combinations, by inducing an impracticability of success. An active commerce, an extensive navigation, a flourishing marine would then be the inevitable offspring of moral and physical necessity. We might defy the little arts of little politicians to control or vary the irresistible and unchangeable course of nature. (11:82)[42]

---

41. "It is a just observation," Hamilton wrote in *The Report on Manufactures* (1791), "that minds of the strongest and most active powers for their proper objects fall below mediocrity and labour without effect, if confined to uncongenial pursuits. And it is thence to be inferred, that the results of human exertion may be immensely increased by diversifying its objects. When all the different kinds of industry obtain in a community, each individual can find his proper element, and can call into activity the whole vigour of his nature. And the community is benefitted by services of respective members, in the manner, in which each can serve it with most effect.... To cherish and stimulate the activity of the human mind, by multiplying the objects of enterprise, is not among the least considerable of the expedients, by which the wealth of a nation may be promoted. Even things in themselves not positively advantageous, sometimes become so, by their tendency to provoke exertion." "Alexander Hamilton's Final Version of the Report on the Subject of Manufactures," in *The Papers of Alexander Hamilton*, ed. Harold C. Syrett and Jacob E. Cooke (New York: Columbia University Press, 1961), Vol. 10, pp. 230, 255–256.

America must pursue this "irresistible and unchangeable course of nature," which Publius in no uncertain terms makes clear is being arrested by "little politicians." Adopting the Constitution would produce what Hamilton, prior to *The Federalist,* had referred to as government that is founded in rational and durable liberty[43] and that will therefore promote innovation, enterprise, responsibility, and technological and military dynamism.

Like today, the question of America's role in the world was front and center for Publius. America could figure prominently in that world, at least if Americans adopted the Constitution. The new constitutional union would enable Americans both in the realm of necessity and in the realm of freedom, providing security while at the same time creating a dynamic republic historically unprecedented in its promotion of those conditions necessary for the flourishing of individual and political liberty.

Union was the predicate for all of this, the means through which American citizenship might be raised above the vain and factious particularities of region, race, creed, and class divisions based on disparities of wealth. The Constitution's union would facilitate the same end as its republicanism: respect for the principles on which the Constitution was based as well as veneration for the Constitution.

---

42. See also *Federalist* 34:204: "[I]f we mean to be a commercial people, it must form a part of our policy to be able one day to defend that commerce. The support of a navy and of naval wars would involve contingencies that must baffle all the efforts of political arithmetic."

43. For Hamilton's early discussion of the concept of rational and durable liberty, see Alexander Hamilton, "The Continentalist No. I," in *The Papers of Alexander Hamilton,* Vol. 2, p. 649 and esp. p. 651. See also McNamara, *Political Economy and Statesmanship,* pp. 96–97.

Chapter 3

REPUBLICANISM

*P*ublius's defense of union and a uniform concept of citizenship was intended to promote a high-toned American nationalism removed from the base and chauvinistic forms of national identity that had typified pre-modern republics and other more illiberal regimes. Publius's defense of the republicanism of the Constitution had similar ends. It was also designed to protect private rights and the general welfare.

The Constitution's republicanism was the means through which political choice could be exercised both wisely and prudently, the vehicle for the exercise of political as opposed to civil or individual liberty. As noted earlier, despite economic interests and passions,[44] the goal of good government under the Constitution was to guide political choice by reason — what has sometimes been referred to as "deliberative democracy." As Publius famously formulated the goal, "it is the reason, alone, of the public, that ought to control and regulate the government. The passions ought to be controlled and regulated by the government." (49:314)

Key to this formulation was not only the concept of *reason*, to which we will turn in a moment, but also that of the *public*, since collectivities are much more difficult to regulate than individuals. Publius points out on a number of occasions that

---

[44] See Kesler, "*Federalist* 10 and American Republicanism."

it is as members of groups that men suffer from the most intractable pathologies and are therefore most ungovernable. Governments are instituted because "the passions of men will not conform to the dictates of reason and justice without constraint"; but the problems arise from men as "bodies" rather than from men as individuals, because it is as bodies that men act with less "rectitude" and "disinterestedness than individuals." There are three reasons for this.

First, reputation "has a less active influence when the infamy of a bad action is to be divided among a number than when it is to fall singly upon one."

Second, the "spirit of faction...is apt to mingle its poison in the deliberations of all bodies of men" such that it "will often hurry the persons of whom they are composed into improprieties and excesses for which they would blush in a private capacity."

Third, there is the problem of "sovereign power," which all collective bodies exercise to a greater or lesser extent. Collectivities tend "to look with an evil eye upon all external attempts to restrain or direct" their "operations." Publius attributes this tendency to "the love of power. Power controlled or abridged is almost always the rival and enemy of that power by which it is controlled or abridged." (15:106)[45]

The purpose of republicanism is to check these factious propensities of collective bodies and to moderate the lack of rectitude or lack of disinterestedness that typifies collectivities. The rule of law requires that laws be made for the general welfare and applicable to all. They should not be made for the benefit of specific constituencies; otherwise, the Constitution's objects of limited government would be transformed into objects of unlimited government, catering to any interests for

---

[45.] See also Epstein, *The Political Theory of The Federalist*, p. 37.

which there is a constituency. Collective bodies have a propensity to pursue their own interests to the exclusion of the general interests of the community.

REPUBLICANISM, NOT "PLURALISM"

The Constitution's goal of promoting the general welfare and the use of the Constitution's republican forms for the pursuit of this end cannot be stressed enough, since many scholars of the Founding argue that the Constitution's republicanism was intended to institutionalize a regime of pluralism in which political interests or preferences compete against one another and law is the outcome of this competition. In this view, congressional policymaking works by aggregating constituency and representative preferences through a variety of bargaining procedures such as log-rolling, side payments, compromise, and other forms of interest exchange with a view to benefiting specific constituencies and preferences.[46] This is not only how laws actually are made, but how Framers like Madison intended them to be made.

So we are told. Nothing, however, could be further from Madison's or Publius's understanding of republicanism under the Constitution.

The pluralist model of representation, which in the 20th century was institutionalized through the growth of the modern regulatory state, has transformed American republicanism into what Theodore Lowi has referred to as "interest-group liberalism," a model of government in which no distinction is made between the political process and the workings of gov-

---

[46.] For a discussion of these bargaining theories of congressional process and their limits, see Joseph M. Bessette, *The Mild Voice of Reason: Deliberative Democracy and American National Government* (Chicago: University of Chicago Press, 1994), esp. pp. 56–66.

ernment: The political process *is* government, and groups are seen as virtuous and in need of accommodation rather than as selfish and in need of regulation.[47]

George Carey has explained similarly that "the most widely shared view of how the American political system operates at the national level" explains it "in terms of a collision of interests where it is assumed that the outcome of the collision accords with the common good largely because of the degree of consensus behind it." However, absent from this standard version of American republicanism are such Madisonian "considerations as 'the true interest' of the country, 'the permanent and aggregate interests of the community,' or the 'general good.'" As much as this orthodox version of American republicanism may provide "an accurate portrayal of the American system in its relevant dimensions, there is little reason to presume that we have a republican government free from the control of factions." In short, "Madison's theory, no matter how one chooses to read it, does not support the notion that the true interests of the country emerge through the resolution of interest conflict."[48]

To the contrary, the very purpose of the representational process under the Constitution was to moderate private interests through the vehicle of representation, to convert private interests into public opinions or public *reason.* This is what Publius meant when he said that "it is the reason, alone, of the public, that ought to control and regulate the government." Republicanism would break down faction by filtering it through representation, and both the institutional mechanisms of the federal government and the elevated character of elected officials would raise political deliberation

---

47. Theodore J. Lowi, *The End of Liberalism: The Second Republic of the United States,* 2nd ed. (New York: W. W. Norton, 1979), pp. 50–58.

to a level higher than the people by themselves could achieve. In this way, the Constitution would respect the people's capacity to choose while simultaneously promoting the principles of good government.

As Publius framed the matter, representation would "refine and enlarge the public views by passing them through the medium of a chosen body of citizens, whose wisdom may best discern the true interest of their country and whose patriotism and love of justice will be least likely to sacrifice it to temporary or partial considerations." (10:76) The emphasis here on the true as opposed to the false or purported interest of the country, and the necessity of inoculating the general welfare against temporary or partial considerations, made it clear that the Constitution was designed to facilitate deliberative, constitutional majorities that would take account of minority interests and rights in pursuit of the common good.

---

48. George W. Carey, *In Defense of the Constitution* (Indianapolis, Ind.: Liberty Fund, 1995), p. 47. See also Lowi, *The End of Liberalism*, p. 58: "To the Madisonian, groups were a necessary evil much in need of regulation. To the modern pluralist, groups are good, requiring only accommodation. Madison went beyond his definition of the group to a position that 'the regulation of these various interfering interests forms the principal task of modern legislation.'" Bessette describes how the dominant theories of congressional process in modern political science have similarly denigrated Madison's understanding of deliberative democracy: "[S]cholars of American government and politics seem increasingly drawn to an analytical framework that sees lawmaking and policymaking as the aggregation of individual interests and preferences—the rational actor, or self-interest, model—and not the result of argument, reasoning, and persuasion about common ends or goals." Bessette, *The Mild Voice of Reason*, p. xi. See also Jeremy Rabkin, *Judicial Compulsions: How Public Law Distorts Public Policy* (New York: Basic Books, 1989), pp.19, 23–26, and 41, and Ward E. Y. Elliott, *The Rise of Guardian Democracy: The Supreme Court's Role in Voting Rights Disputes, 1845–1969* (Cambridge, Mass.: Harvard University Press, 1974), pp. 7–8.

As difficult as it might be to achieve a consensus on what defined the public good—and, admittedly, this is seldom easy—abandoning this standard as the guiding light for public reasoning on what the law should be would reduce government to chaos, with an unceasing clash of particular interests making unending demands on the public purse. This, of course, largely defines the modern programmatic liberal state that American government has become.

MAJORITY INTEREST IS NOT ALWAYS THE PUBLIC GOOD

It is important to note that, although the republican principle of majority rule would be respected under the Constitution, majority rule was not synonymous with majority interests. "When a majority is included in a faction," Publius declared, the very "form of popular government...enables it to sacrifice to its ruling passion or interest both the public good and the rights of other citizens." It was "[t]o secure the public good and private rights against the danger of such a faction, and at the same time to preserve the spirit and form of popular government" that the inquiries in *The Federalist* and, more generally, the Constitution itself were directed. (10:75) The implications of these compact passages are many, but for our purposes, two are particularly important.

First, since minority faction can be defeated in popular government through elections and majority faction cannot, it is especially the latter form of faction that the Constitution must guard against. Because the basis of American constitutionalism is the individual and the object of legislative process is the general welfare or public interest, the Constitution's republican forms—its bicameralism, different terms of elections, separation of powers, checks and balances, and other institutional mechanisms—were intended above all to defeat majority factions.

Second, since the majority's ruling passions and interests were not synonymous with the public good and were in fact its antithesis,[49] the public good was obviously something distinct from mere particular passions or interests, including the majority's passions or interests.[50] This is rarely appreciated in political science and the legal academic literature on the Founders' republicanism, as the remarks of Lowi and Carey make clear. However much passions or interests might animate political actors, be they part of the majority or minority, it was the specific purpose of federal institutional process, according to Publius, to wean representatives from those interests to which they were drawn so passionately.

Key here were not merely the Constitution's institutional processes, but its limited objects, both of which would work to

---

[49.] Madison emphasizes this point in the first paragraph of *Federalist* 10: "Complaints are everywhere heard from our most considerate and virtuous citizens, equally the friends of public and private faith and of public and personal liberty, that our governments are too unstable, that the public good is disregarded in the conflicts of rival parties, and that measures are too often decided, not according to the rules of justice and the rights of the minor party, but by the superior force of an interested and overbearing majority." *Federalist* 10:72.

[50.] In a letter to Thomas Jefferson dated October 17, 1788, Madison remarked: "Wherever the real power in a Government lies, there is the danger of oppression. In our Governments the real power lies in the majority of the community, and the invasion of private rights is *chiefly* to be apprehended, not from acts of Government contrary to the sense of its constituents, but from acts in which the Government is the mere instrument of the major number of the Constituents. This is a truth of great importance, but not yet sufficiently attended to." In *The Mind of the Founder: Sources of the Political Thought of James Madison,* ed. with intro. and commentary Marvin Meyers (Hanover, Md.: Brandeis University Press, 1981), p. 157; emphasis in original.

raise deliberations from mere interests to what would promote the general welfare.[51] James Buchanan and Roger Congleton have referred to this type of republicanism as "politics by principle, not interest."[52] However one characterizes it, Publius's republicanism poses problems for political observers and advocates who would reduce politics to a mere clash of interests in which it is necessary, as *Federal Farmer VII* argued, to represent all classes in society and to allow electors to "chuse men from among themselves, and genuinely like themselves."[53]

Such an argument, as Publius demonstrated initially in *Federalist* 35 and later in *Federalists* 55 and 56, misapprehended the nature of American republicanism. Representing all classes and all interests in society was both impracticable and unnecessary. It was impracticable because it was impossible to represent all interests in any representative body.[54] This was especially true in the large republic envisioned by the Constitu-

---

[51.] See *Federalist* 60: 365–366: "There is sufficient diversity in the state of property, in the genius, manners, and habits of the people of the different parts of the Union to occasion a material diversity of disposition in their representatives towards the different ranks and conditions in society. And though an intimate intercourse under the same government will promote a gradual assimilation of temper and sentiments, yet there are causes, as well physical as moral, which may, in a greater or less degree, permanently nourish different propensities and inclinations in this particular. But the circumstance which will be likely to have the greatest influence in the matter will be the dissimilar modes of constituting the several component parts of the government. The House of Representatives being to be elected immediately by the people, the Senate by the State legislatures, the President by electors chosen for that purpose by the people, there would be little probability of a common interest to cement these different branches in a predilection for any particular class of electors."

[52.] James M. Buchanan and Roger D. Congleton, *Politics by Principle, Not Interest: Toward Nondiscriminatory Democracy*, Vol. 11 of *The Collected Works of James M. Buchanan* (Indianapolis: Liberty Fund, 2003).

tion. It was unnecessary because the objects of the federal government were limited to commerce, finance, military affairs,
treaties, and other forms of "negotiation," all of which would
be pursued with a view to the common good, not narrow constituent interests. (17:114; 36:344) An election was not about
representing interests or capturing every shade of public opinion. It was, rather, about judging the character and opinions of
a representative and about selecting a government that was the
best available:

> The aim of every political constitution is, or
> ought to be, first to obtain for rulers men who
> possess most wisdom to discern, and most virtue
> to pursue, the common good of the society; and
> in the next place, to take the most effectual pre-
> cautions for keeping them virtuous whilst they
> continue to hold their public trust. (57:348)

The difficult question, as Publius emphasized in *Federalist*
56, was not so much ensuring that representatives were familiar with local interests, but rather that they had a sufficiently

---

53. The Federal Farmer VII, in *The Anti-Federalist: Writings by the Opponents of the Constitution*, ed. Herbert J. Storing, selected by Murray Dry (Chi-cago: University of Chicago Press, 1985), pp. 73, 75. Melancton Smith made a similar argument at the New York Ratifying Conven-tion, June 20–21, 1788. See *The Founders' Constitution*, eds. Philip B. Kurland and Ralph Lerner (Indianapolis, Ind.: Liberty Fund, 1987), Vol. I, p. 410.
54. As Hannah Pitkin notes, the mirror concept of representation, like that suggested by the Anti-Federalists, may require selection of candi-dates by lottery or random sampling if the ideal of representing as many segments or "classes" in society is to be achieved. See Hanna Fenichel Pitkin, *The Concept of Representation* (Berkeley: University of California Press, 1972), p. 73. See also Will Kymlicka, *Multicultural Citizenship: A Liberal Theory of Minority Rights* (New York: Oxford Univer-sity Press, 1997), p. 139.

general knowledge of other states and matters that they could pass laws with a view to the general welfare. Members of Congress were expected to be familiar with local interests, but they were not expected to be lobbyists for them, a point Madison stressed not only in *The Federalist*, but also in a 1785 letter to Thomas Jefferson in which he assailed members of the Continental Congress for acting like "advocates for the respective interests of their constituents."[55]

Publius's remarks here are contradictory of today's scholarship on congressional process, which frequently defends the idea that Members of Congress should act as suppliants or "rent seekers" for specific constituent interests, and of Congress's and the Supreme Court's own understanding of republicanism under the Constitution. Section 2 of the Voting Rights Act, for instance, codifies a right of minorities to "elect their candidate of choice" to office in federal and state elections. For over a generation, the Court has interpreted the VRA to provide an entitlement to racial officeholding in which it is expected that Members of Congress elected from racially configured electoral districts mandated by the VRA will act on behalf of racial constituencies.

[55.] To Thomas Jefferson, Philada. Octr. 3, 1785, in *The Papers of James Madison, Vol. 8, 10 March 1784–28 March 1786*, eds. Robert A. Rutland, William M.E. Rachal, Barbara D. Ripel, and Fredrika J. Trute (Chicago: University of Chicago Press, 1973), pp. 373, 374. See also *Federalist* 46:302–303: "What is the spirit that has in general characterized the proceedings of Congress? A perusal of their journals, as well as the candid acknowledgments of such as have had a seat in that assembly, will inform us, that the members have but too frequently displayed the character, rather of partisans of their respective States, than of impartial guardians of a common interest; that where on one occasion improper sacrifices have been made of local considerations, to the aggrandizement of the federal government, the great interests of the nation have suffered on a hundred, from an undue attention to the local prejudices, interests, and views of the particular States."

Such an understanding is inconsistent with the republicanism of the Constitution because it suggests that Members of
Congress should act on behalf of particular or special interests
rather than on behalf of the public or general interest. It is also
illiberal because those particular interests that Members of
Congress are expected to represent also happen to be *racial*
interests. Not only does VRA jurisprudence incite the faction
that Publius suggests is synonymous with all types of particular or special-interest legislation, but it does so on the basis of
the spring of action that both Publius and the Constitution
suggest may be the most inflammatory of all: *race*.[56]

[56.] In his famous Convention speech of June 6, 1787, the precursor to
Federalist 10, Madison noted how religion could "become a motive to
persecution & oppression" and that "We have seen the mere distinction of colour made in the midst of the most enlightened period of
time, a ground of the most oppressive dominion ever exercised by man
over man." James Madison, speech at the Constitutional Convention,
June 6, 1787, in Farrand, *Records of the Federal Convention*, Vol. I, p. 135.
It was not just religious classifications that Madison thought might
promote oppression and social disintegration. Race classifications
were equally ominous. Prophetically, perhaps, in *Federalist* 17 Publius
offers the example of Scotland's "incorporation with England" (into
the United Kingdom) as an example of how Scotland's "fierce and
ungovernable" "spirit of clanship" was subdued and rendered subordinate to "a more rational and more energetic system of civil polity."
Federalist 17:117. Congress and the Supreme Court today have apparently forgotten this instructive example of how union—and, specifically, American union—might provide a similar remedy for today's
divisive politics of ethnoracial identity. For a critique of how the
Supreme Court's voting rights jurisprudence has undermined the
Founders' republicanism, and specifically the republicanism of *The Federalist*, see Anthony A. Peacock, *Deconstructing the Republic: Voting Rights, the
Supreme Court, and the Founders' Republicanism Reconsidered* (Washington,
D.C.: AEI Press, 2008).

Chapter 4

SEPARATION OF POWERS

Succinctly put, separation of powers as defended in *The Federalist* has two goals or purposes. The first is negative: the protection of individual liberty from possible injustices by political officials. The second, often overlooked, is positive: Separation of powers creates a division of labor that allows each branch to be organized in a way that best enables it to fulfill its unique function. In other words, the separation of powers doctrine is based on a functional distinction between the expertise and capacity of the various branches of government as much as it is on a political anthropology that seeks to counteract ambition with ambition. (*51*:317–322)[57]

Today, the federal government's regime of positive rights or entitlements has exposed it to capture by specific interests. Contrary to the original goal of separation of powers, the objects of government are no longer public goods but private goods: the goods of specific groups or individuals.

Publius ends the first half of *The Federalist* (*Federalists* 1–36) by proclaiming that it will be "happy" for Americans and "most honorable for human nature" if Americans have "wisdom and virtue enough" to adopt the Constitution. (*36*:220) He then proceeds in the introduction to the second half (*Feder-*

---

57. See also Donald L. Horowitz, *The Courts and Social Policy* (Washington, D.C.: The Brookings Institution, 1977), pp. 18–19.

alist 37) to declare that a more exacting analysis of the Constitution than what has been provided so far is needed.

In particular, the "theoretical propriety" of the Constitution needs to be examined and defended. As much as the Convention had to accommodate "the force of extraneous considerations" (37:226), especially the conflicting claims of different-sized states and the differing interests that the Convention had to recognize, Publius contends that the Constitution remains highly defensible as a work of political and constitutional theory. The "wisdom and virtue" of Americans and the honor of "human nature" seem to consist in recognizing the theoretical propriety of the Constitution and adopting it for that reason, thus affirming again that men are capable of establishing government from "reflection and choice" rather than "accident and force."

THE THEORY OF SEPARATION OF POWERS

A critical element of the Constitution's new theory is its separation of powers. As Publius emphasizes in *Federalist* 37, "past experience" under the Articles of Confederation had revealed just how "fallacious" its principles were, and it was necessary to "change this first foundation, and with it the superstructure resting upon it." (37:222) The two most critical elements of that superstructure will be the separation of powers and federalism.

The principles that will need to be changed involve the relationship between republicanism and the separation of powers. The Constitution is republican in form, by which Publius means it "derives all its powers directly or indirectly from the great body of the people." (39:237) But that republican form, as Publius highlights, can undermine stability and energy in government. Stability requires that laws not be changed often, which in turn requires those in government to possess power for a length of time. Energy requires the execution of power by a single hand. The principles of republicanism, which seem to require that power be held for a short duration and by multiple hands, are opposed to stability and energy in government. (37:223)

The separation of powers under the Constitution will remedy these defects of republicanism. In *Federalist* 10, republicanism is defended as the savior of popular sovereignty. In *Federalists* 47–51, however, Publius provides a contrasting account, portraying republicanism as something that, unmoderated by the Constitution's separation of powers, introduces dangers against which Americans need to be on guard.

Publius opens *Federalist* 47 by declaring: "The accumulation of all powers, legislative, executive, and judiciary, in the same hands, whether of one, a few, or many, and whether hereditary, self-appointed, or elective, may justly be pronounced the very definition of tyranny." (47:298) The legislative, executive, and judicial powers of government must therefore be properly separated if tyranny is not to occur. This is as true of popular governments as it is of hereditary or self-appointed governments.

Then comes the revelation about the danger of republicanism: "The legislative department," Publius proclaims, "is everywhere extending the sphere of its activity and drawing all power into its impetuous vortex." (48:306) It is the legislative branch of government—that most popular branch, closest to the people—that is the greatest danger to republics, including the American confederation. Yet this is a danger that is natural to republics because republics are popular governments.

Federalists 47 and 48 illustrate that the government of the Confederation, like many state governments, is subject to imperious control by legislatures that have undermined stability and energy in government. *Federalists* 49 and 50 add that, as much as the Constitution is anchored in popular consent, the only legitimate fountain of governmental authority, "recurrence to the people" for "keeping the several departments of power within their constitutional limits" (49:311) on either an occasional or a periodical basis—the solutions of Thomas Jefferson and Pennsylvania's Council of Censors, respectively—would not work to preserve the separation of powers. Occasional appeals to the people, for instance, would undermine respect for the Constitution because its provisions would be perpetually altered; would disturb the public tranquility by unleashing public passions in frequent, hotly contested disputes over the proper separation of powers; and would likely result in a further aggrandizement of legislative power, since "the tendency of republican governments is to an aggrandizement of the legislative at the expense of the other departments." (49:312)

Accordingly, if the "fallacious" principles on which the Articles were based are to be abandoned, something more will have to be done. The "interior structure of the government" (51:317–318) will have to be modified in such a way as to create separate executive and judicial departments that will have significant powers and independence. *Federalists* 48–50 demonstrate that mere "parchment barriers" (48:305) (written limitations within a constitution) or "recurrence to the people" are insufficient to maintain a proper separation of powers. *Federalist* 51 offers a solution.

In *Federalist* 51, Publius makes three "general observations" about what is needed for the separation of powers to be effective. First, each branch of the federal government "should have a will of its own," meaning that "each should have as little agency as possible in the appointment of members of the others." Lack of agency over the other branches of government will preserve a certain freedom of will for those other departments that is essential to maintaining their separate powers. But Publius adds that:

> Some deviations [from this principle] must be admitted. In the constitution of the judiciary department in particular, it might be inexpedient to insist rigorously on the principle: first, because peculiar qualifications being essential in the members, the primary consideration ought to be to select that mode of choice which best secures these qualifications; second, because the permanent tenure by which the appointments are held in that department must soon destroy all sense of dependence on the authority conferring them. (51:318)

Publius singles out the judiciary for special treatment. Here, it appears that the idea of separate wills for each department of the federal government must be abandoned, at least temporarily, because the primary consideration in selecting judges has to be their qualifications. The means of choosing judges must therefore be limited to those that best secure these qualifications. Apparently, considerations of excellence and liberty trump considerations of equality. There are multiple principles at work in the Constitution, and what best promotes liberty and good government must supersede any pure principles of equality or republicanism.

Nevertheless, Publius's second point—that the permanent tenure of judicial appointments means that those appointed will soon lose any "sense of dependence on the authority conferring them"—affirms that the principle of each department having a will of its own will be preserved, at least sometime "soon" after the judicial appointment is made, under the Constitution. Despite being nominated by the President and confirmed by the Senate, members of the federal judiciary will eventually lose any sense of dependence on these branches of the federal government, and Publius's first principle will be maintained.

The second observation Publius invokes in defense of the Constitution's separation of powers is that "the members of each department should be as little dependent as possible on those of the others for the emoluments annexed to their offices." (51:318) Publius emphasizes that the real danger here lies in Congress controlling the salaries of the executive and the judiciary. If the executive or federal judiciary were "not independent of the legislature in this particular, their independence in every other would be merely nominal." (51:318) This principle is a corollary of the first principle, since a department will not have a separate will if its remuneration can be controlled by Congress.

Finally, "the great security against a gradual concentration of the several powers in the same department consists in giving to those who administer each department the necessary constitutional means and personal motives to resist encroachments of the others." Giving members of the different branches the constitutional means and personal motives to protect themselves is the most important safeguard against the accumulation of all powers in a single branch. Publius adds that the "provision for defense must in this, as in all other cases, be made commensurate to the danger of attack. Ambition must be made to counteract ambition. The interest of the man must be connected with the constitutional rights of the place." (51:318–319) The constitutional means to secure separation of powers must allow members of each branch to exercise personal motives, specifically motives of ambition, which Publius makes clear will tie the interest of the man to the constitutional rights of the place.

In other words, it is not interest alone or interest unadulterated that will guide the actors in each branch of the federal government. Rather, it is interest modified by an ambition that will induce officials to protect the constitutional rights of their offices.

HOW DOES *THE FEDERALIST* TREAT AMBITION?

Ambition is an ambiguous term that appears to mean not merely the love of power, but a desire to be publicly recognized, particularly for good deeds. For instance, in *Federalist* 72, where Publius discusses presidential re-eligibility, he defines the "love of fame" as "the ruling passion of the noblest minds." (72:436) Even the noblest minds are ruled by passion, but it is a passion to do good: The noblest minds seek fame, not infamy.

In *Federalist* 51, Publius does not suggest that such noble intentions are the basis of maintaining the separation of powers. To the contrary, he refers to his imperative of ambition counteracting ambition as a "policy of supplying, by opposite and rival interests, the *defect* of better motives." (51:319; emphasis added)

It is worth noting, however, that although the separation of powers doctrine in *Federalist* 51 is predicated on defective motives, it does not preclude the exercise of higher or "better" motives in preserving the constitutional rights of each branch of government. Ambition to do good—specifically, to protect the constitutional rights of not only one's own department, but perhaps even the departments of others as a matter of constitutional *principle* rather than simply as a matter of constitutional *turf*—is not precluded by *Federalist* 51.

AN INDEPENDENT JUDICIARY

This is especially important in the case of the judiciary. Publius warns that "it is not possible to give to each department an equal power of self-defense" and that since, in "republican government, the legislative authority necessarily predominates," the remedy for this problem "is to divide the legislature into different branches; and to render them, by different modes of election and different principles of action, as little connected with each other as the nature of their common functions and their common dependence on the society will admit." (51:319) This explains the bicameralism of Congress, which will work to secure the separation of powers by protecting the executive and judicial branches of government from the legislature.

But what about protecting the legislative and executive branches from the judiciary? It is not only the legislature that must be accounted for in providing "each department an equal power of self defence." The legislative and executive must also be protected from the judiciary because that branch of the federal government is particularly immune to the principle of ambition checking ambition. The reason stems from the nature of judicial review; that is, the power of federal courts to review legislative acts for their potential constitutional infirmity, a power that may have been of little consequence during the era of *The Federalist* but that looms large in today's politics.

Publius clearly contemplates the power of judicial review. In *Federalist* 39, for instance, he outlines that "the tribunal" to resolve federalism disputes—boundary disputes between the federal and state governments—must "be established under the general government" and that judicial resolution of such conflicts is necessary in order to avoid "an appeal to the sword and a dissolution of the compact." (39:242) In *Federalist* 78, Publius declares that a "limited Constitution," "one which

contains certain specified exceptions to the legislative authority," requires an independent judiciary. Without an independent judiciary to check legislative power, "all the reservations
of particular rights or privileges would amount to nothing."
(78:465)

What happens, however, when the Constitution succeeds
in making the judiciary "independent" of the legislature and
the executive? Unlike these latter branches, which are elected
for terms, federal judges are appointed for life. Accordingly,
once they attain office, there is no way for the ambition of
Congress or the ambition of the President to check them. In
other words, the principle of ambition counteracting ambition
does not apply in the case of the federal judiciary because it is
maintained by a different principle that does not rely on "the
defect of better motives" so much as on those *better motives* themselves. Federal courts must exercise *self*-restraint rather than be
restrained by *others* in Publius's constitutional system. They
must be motivated by their devotion to constitutional *principle*
rather than by the baser motives of protecting and enlarging
their own judicial *turf* if the separation of powers is to be
maintained.

This can certainly work as long as federal judges act
within their constitutional boundaries. Publius suggests that
the principal constitutional role of the federal judiciary will be
to protect individual rights from encroachment by the political
branches of government. There may be some federalism disputes to resolve at times (although likely very few), but "political questions" will generally remain for the political branches
of government, not the judiciary, to resolve. If the principal
role of the judiciary is, then, to defend individual rights against
political overreach, the precondition for this is that the judiciary itself not engage in political disputes or decision-making.
It must remain politically separate if it is to arbitrate neutrally

on questions of rights.[58] As Publius puts it, "the general liberty of the people can never be endangered" by the courts "*so long* as the judiciary remains truly distinct from both the legislature and the executive." (78:464–465; emphasis added)

But what happens when the judiciary no longer remains truly distinct from the legislature and the executive? Today's federal judiciary, and the Supreme Court in particular, exercises control over virtually all important political disputes in America. The courts may not be institutionally tied to Congress or the President, but they exercise a broad array of political powers that the Founders, including Publius, never contemplated to be within the purview of the federal courts to control.

Article I, Section 4 of the Constitution, for instance, makes it clear that only the states or Congress can regulate the time, places, or manner of congressional elections. Yet beginning in 1962, the Supreme Court determined that, despite this clear constitutional language, it had the power to assess questions of "fair" representation and reapportionment.[59] The federal courts also routinely decide how prisons and schools should be managed and even how taxpayers' money should be spent on these public institutions. Are these clearly not political questions best left for the legislative and executive branches of government to resolve? Recently, the Supreme Court has decided that it, not Congress or the President, has the final say over war policy and, specifically, the proper balance between individual rights and national security concerns.[60] In numerous other areas of public policy, the Court now has the final say.

[58.] See Gordon S. Wood, *The Radicalism of the American Revolution* (New York: Alfred A. Knopf, 1992), pp. 324–325.

[59.] *Baker v. Carr*, 369 U.S. 186 (1962).

[60.] See *Hamdi v. Rumsfeld*, 542 U.S. 507 (2004).

In the wake of such clear political decision-making by federal courts, how can the judiciary be reined in and the separation of powers maintained? There seems to be little constitutional remedy for such a problem, since impeachment of federal judges is not available for erroneous decision-making, but only for treason, bribery, and other high crimes and misdemeanors.[61]

Publius clearly understood that the power of judicial review had to depend on the exercise of judicial self-restraint, an exception to *Federalist* 51's imperative of departmental ambition counteracting departmental ambition. This anomaly in the separation of powers doctrine, which seeks to place the power of reconciling majoritarian rule and minority rights in a nonpolitical, largely unaccountable institution, the judiciary—what has been referred to as the "Madisonian Dilemma"[62]—was for the most part irrelevant until the mid-20th century. Today, however, it remains a perennial problem in American constitutionalism.

A STRONG EXECUTIVE

Finally, as I have noted, not just the judiciary, but also the executive needs to be fortified to check the legislative branch. One of the most significant contributions *The Federalist* made to the history of political thought was its discussion of how the Constitution republicanized the executive.[63]

A constant theme throughout *The Federalist* was the necessity for more energetic government, an imperative that was to

---

61. Constitution of the United States, Article II, Section 4.

62. See Robert H. Bork, *The Tempting of America: The Political Seduction of the Law* (New York: Touchstone, 1990), pp. 139–141.

63. See Harvey C. Mansfield, *Taming the Prince: The Ambivalence of Modern Executive Power* (Baltimore: Johns Hopkins University Press, 1993), esp. Ch. 10, "Republicanizing the Executive," pp. 247–278.

be carried out above all by the executive. In *Federalist* I, Publius warned that "An enlightened zeal for the energy and efficiency of government will be stigmatized as the offspring of a temper fond of despotic power and hostile to the principles of liberty." (1:29) In other words, those like Publius who advocated more energetic government in America—and under the Constitution more particularly—would be denounced by the Constitution's critics as giving the government too much power, which would be used to crush individual liberties.

Publius's counter was that without such power, the very liberties that the Constitution's critics were so desperate to protect would themselves be jeopardized. Had this not been the case with the Confederation, where the government's weakness jeopardized such individual liberties as property rights and rights of contract? Publius warned that it was too easily "forgotten that the vigor of government is essential to the security of liberty." (1:29)

If government needs power to secure liberty, how much power is needed? Publius's response was that it would require power adequate to whatever necessities confronted the national government in domestic and foreign affairs. Perhaps the most astonishing statement in the entire *Federalist* was the declaration in *Federalist* 23 that the powers necessary for the common defense "ought to exist without limitation, *because it is impossible to foresee or to define the extent and variety of national exigencies, and the correspondent extent and variety of the means which may be necessary to satisfy them.*"(23:149; emphasis in original)[64] America's enemies define the extent of the powers necessary for self-defense. To limit these powers in the Constitution would thus be suicidal.

But if the federal government was a government of limited powers, how were unlimited national defense powers to be reconciled with a Constitution of limited, enumerated objects? Part of the answer lay in the four-year term and popular control of the executive. A unitary executive in particular, as opposed to a plural executive, would facilitate responsible government because it would make very clear who was at fault when bad executive decisions were made. If the voters did not like the actions a President took, they could dispatch him and his Administration at the end of his four-year term. Unity was "conducive to energy" in the executive because it facilitated "[d]ecision, activity, secrecy, and dispatch," but it was especially important to "the conduct of war," where energy in the executive was "the bulwark of the national security." (70:422–423, 425)

In a democratic regime like America's, the necessity of a unitary executive was difficult to accept because of the "maxim of republican jealousy which considers power as safer in the hands of a number of men than of a single man." (70:428) Publius sought to educate the American people on the imperative of recognizing the limits that necessity, particularly in national security, places on republicanism and political choice.[65] As he stressed in *Federalist* 70, in the case of the executive branch, the multiplication of officeholders was "rather dangerous than friendly to liberty." (70:428) Today, of course, we have divided the executive power by vesting it in dozens of officials housed in separate administrative agencies, many of which are entirely independent of the chief executive.

[64.] See also *Federalist* 34.203: "Constitutions of civil government are not to be framed upon a calculation of existing exigencies, but upon a combination of these with the probable exigencies of ages, according to the natural and tried course of human affairs. Nothing, therefore, can be more fallacious than to infer the extent of any power proper to be lodged in the national government from an estimate of its immediate necessities. There ought to be a CAPACITY to provide for future contingencies as they may happen; and as these are illimitable in their nature, so it is impossible safely to limit that capacity."

[65.] See Mansfield, *Taming the Prince*, pp. 255–257.

Republican excess was also the reason for the presidential veto. A unitary executive was necessary not merely for purposes of national security, but also to restrain the legislature and facilitate deliberative republicanism. In his commentary on the executive, Publius again warned of the dangers in republics of those governing capitulating "to every sudden breeze of passion" or "transient impulse" and of the "propensity of the legislative department to intrude upon the rights, and to absorb the powers, of the other departments." Publius saw the presidential veto both as "a shield to the executive" and as a means of furnishing "an additional security against the enaction of improper laws."(71:430, 73:441)

Indeed, as yet another element of *The Federalist*'s high politics, Publius saw in the separation of powers generally and the presidency more particularly the potential for the exercise of virtue. As Harvey Mansfield has noted, the Constitution's executive was designed to attract to the national government the "noblest minds." These preeminent individuals might restrain the excesses of lawmaking to which all republican legislatures were prone and, in their unitary control of the executive, exercise not only prudence in the preservation of national security, but also wisdom and innovation in carrying the nation to new heights through executive leadership. The executive thus provided one more avenue through which America's potential for national and civilizational greatness could be advanced.[66]

[66.] See *ibid.*, esp. pp. 259–272.

Chapter 5

FEDERALISM

F or Publius, federalism was a crucial principle without which liberty would be lost. The extended sphere was impossible without federalism because local political freedom would be lost without it. The title of *The Federalist* itself made clear that Publius intended to defend the Constitution's consistency with federalism against the accusations of the Anti-Federalists that the Constitution would instead concentrate political power and destroy America's federal structure of government.

Moreover, federalism was a part of the separation of powers. This is not often noted by readers of *The Federalist*. In *Federalist* 51, Publius added to his three general observations about the separation of powers "two considerations" about America's federal system that "place that system in a very interesting point of view." The first was the fact of federalism: the division of political power into state and federal governments, which made America a "compound republic" and provided "a double security...to the rights of the people." The second was the extended sphere: the large size of the American union that would incorporate so many economic and social interests, as well as religious sects, that the size of the country on its own would serve "to guard one part of the society against the injustice of the other part." (51:320)

A BETTER FORM OF FEDERALISM: PUBLIUS VS. THE ANTI-FEDERALISTS

The problem with the kind of federalism advocated by the Anti-Federalists, who merely sought to maintain the loose confederation of the Articles, was that state governments under the Articles were factious, governed by petty, self-interested elites. This was true even of the larger states within the Union. Without the necessary modifications that the Constitution would bring to the federal structure of government, federalism itself would be lost in America.

But if federalism needed the extended sphere to avoid disintegration from the centrifugal forces of overbearing state governments, America also needed a strong central government. In *Federalist* 39, Publius made clear that the Constitution was strictly *republican* in form but not strictly *federal* in form. Rather, it was a *combination* of federal and national elements.

Publius examined five items in this regard: the manner in which the Constitution was ratified; the sources from which the powers of the legislative and executive branches were drawn (that is, the manner in which these bodies were elected); the fact that national powers would operate directly on individuals, not on states (as was the case under the Confederation); the extent or jurisdiction of the national government's powers, which applied to a limited number of enumerated objects only; and the process for amending the Constitution outlined in Article V. He concluded:

> In its foundation [the Constitution] is federal, not national; in the sources from which the ordinary powers of the government are drawn, it is partly federal and partly national; in the operation of these powers, it is national, not federal; in the extent of them, again, it is federal, not

national; and, finally, in the authoritative mode of introducing amendments, it is neither wholly federal nor wholly national. (39:242–243)

The modification of America's federal form by these national elements of the Constitution was necessary to save federalism in America, but Publius suggested that his observations were not reserved to America alone. These modifications to the federal principle would be necessary to save federalism in *any* form of government from dissolution.

Under the Articles, which required the unanimous consent of all the states for the implementation of any federal initiatives, the Confederation was facing "impending anarchy." America's "ambassadors abroad," Publius animadverted, were "mere pageants of mimic sovereignty." Publius further denounced the Confederation as a "league" rather than a "government." Indeed, the Confederation was "incompatible" with the very "idea of GOVERNMENT." Why? Because "[g]overnment implies the power of making laws," and

> It is essential to the idea of a law that it be attended with a sanction; or, in other words, a penalty or punishment for disobedience.... This penalty, whatever it may be, can only be inflicted in two ways: by the agency of the courts and ministers of justice, or by military force; by the COERCION of the magistracy, or by the COERCION of arms. The first kind can evidently apply only to men; the last kind must of necessity, be employed against bodies politic, or communities, or States.

The Confederation was not a government, among other reasons, because it had no coercive power—the power to apply a "sanction" or a "penalty." Even if it did have such power, the

Confederation would be consumed in perpetual war with its composite states because, unlike individuals to whom the laws of the Confederation could not apply, states are "bodies politic" that can resist "the coercion of the magistracy" in a way that individuals cannot. As Publius put it:

> In an association where the general authority is confined to the collective bodies of the communities that compose it, every breach of the laws must involve a state of war; and military execution must become the only instrument of civil obedience. Such a state of things can certainly not deserve the name of government, nor would any prudent man choose to commit his happiness to it. (*15*:101–105)

Without the power to apply its laws directly to individuals, the federal government would be politically ineffective and would literally have to go to war to get its initiatives implemented. This was not only bad government. It was not government at all. But it was how "government" operated under the Articles of Confederation.

The federal principle of the Articles, accordingly, had to be modified. It was Publius's hope that applying federal laws directly to American citizens would not only cause the national government to become more effective and energetic, but also lead Americans eventually to feel a connection to the national government. This, however, would take time.

A FEDERAL SYSTEM OF LIMITED, ENUMERATED POWERS

Publius assured his readers that the federal government's "jurisdiction extends to certain enumerated objects only, and leaves to the several states a residuary and inviolable sovereignty over all other objects." (39:242) In *Federalist* 32, he was more specific:

> [A]s the plan of the convention aims only at a partial union or consolidation, the State governments would clearly retain all the rights of sovereignty which they before had, and which were not, by that act, *exclusively* delegated to the United States. This exclusive delegation, or rather this alienation, of State sovereignty would only exist in three cases: where the Constitution in express terms granted an exclusive authority to the Union; where it granted in one instance an authority to the Union, and in another prohibited the States from exercising the like authority; and where it granted an authority to the Union to which a similar authority in the States would be absolutely and totally *contradictory* and *repugnant*. (32:194; emphasis in original)

Publius sought in these statements to reassure Americans of the limited powers of the national government, but he also saw such limited powers as the corollary of good government. The jack of all trades is a master of none, and it was precisely because the federal government was a limited government that it would be competent to execute the powers it had. Moreover, there was a natural division between state and federal powers, and the latter were few in number.

Federal powers were also more significant, politically speaking, than state powers and thus would likely draw the most ambitious minds to federal politics. In Publius's words, the objects of the federal government fell "less immediately under the observation of the mass of the citizens," so the benefits derived from federal office would "chiefly be perceived and attended to by speculative men" who presumably were of a more philosophic disposition. The frequently menial quality of state powers provided little incentive to federal politicians to encroach on state prerogatives.

> The regulation of the mere domestic police of a State appears to me to hold out slender allurements to ambition. Commerce, finance, negotiation, and war seem to comprehend all the objects which have charms for minds governed by that passion; and all the powers necessary to those objects ought, in the first instance, to be lodged in the national depository. The administration of private justice between the citizens of the same State, the supervision of agriculture and of other concerns of a similar nature, all those things, in short, which are proper to be provided for by local legislation, can never be desirable cares of a general jurisdiction.

The politically most ambitious might find little allure in state politics, but the people would have a natural allegiance to state legislators. Publius concluded that state governments, to the extent that they were well administered, would possess a "greater degree of influence" over the people. The "nature of the objects" of state administration, above all "the ordinary administration of criminal and civil justice," which was "the immediate and visible guardian of life and property," affecting the most "personal interests and familiar concerns" of the people, insured that the state governments rather than the national government would attract the people's "affection, esteem, and reverence." This would hold, however, only so long as the federal government did not offer up a "much better administration" than the states. (*17*:114–116)[67]

It was therefore incumbent on the state governments to administer their affairs well if they wished to retain the sympathy of their citizens. This was the principle of competition applied to governments, and the reward for just behavior was the confidence of the citizenry.

---

67. See also David Broyles, "Federalism and Political Life," in Kesler, *Saving the Revolution*, pp. 76–79.

CONCLUSION

*T*he sort of "feudal anarchy" or "spirit of clanship" (17:116, 117) that Publius feared might overtake America in the late 1700s if overbearing state governments were to prevail has certainly been eclipsed by a national government that has grown in size beyond anything Publius could have imagined. Although there are things today like the politics of multiculturalism and legislation like the current Voting Rights Act, which requires states to create race-based electoral districts, that may foment precisely that spirit of clanship or balkanization that Publius feared,[68] it is equally evident that Publius's anticipation of a growing national identity has come to fruition; Americans today generally

---

[68.] In *Shaw v. Reno*, where the Court reviewed a constitutional challenge to racial redistricting in North Carolina undertaken under the auspices of the Voting Rights Act, the Court warned that "[r]acial gerrymandering, even for remedial purposes, may balkanize us into competing racial factions." *Shaw v. Reno*, 113 S.Ct. 2816 (1993), at 2832. One year later, in *Holder v. Hall*, where the VRA was again in issue, Justice Thomas criticized "vote dilution" law under the act, remarking in his concurring opinion that the legislation fomented racial faction because, as judicially construed, it required states and other jurisdictions to create race-based "political homelands." *Holder v. Hall*, 114 S. Ct. 2581 (1994), at 2598.

identify more with the federal government than they do with their state governments.

Publius's federalism and separation of powers doctrines, like the other elements of his constitutionalism as outlined above, were largely successful, proving both the prophetic and prudential quality of his theory; but it is equally certain that the separation of powers and federalism as outlined in *The Federalist* have been largely surpassed by today's federal administrative state. Various explanations, which cannot be discussed in detail here, may explain these developments.

- For instance, the Seventeenth Amendment, which popularized the election of Senators, arguably removed the only significant check on behalf of state interests from federal institutional process, thus opening the floodgates to the federal regulatory state, which was now free to have its way over a host of areas of American life that previously fell within the jurisdiction of traditional state governmental functions or were left free of regulation altogether in the private world.

- Another common explanation for the growth in the federal government is that in the 1930s the Supreme Court, contrary to Publius's admonitions in *Federalist* 39, abandoned all pretense of policing the boundaries between state and federal powers. Accordingly, Congress was given yet another carte blanche to regulate prerogatives otherwise left to the states by the Constitution, and this under the pretext of the Constitution's Commerce Clause and Necessary and Proper Clause.

Although many other explanations have been offered for the eclipse of the Founders' Constitution by the ideological movements of the 20th century—a development that today seems to be galloping along at a breakneck pace—the Constitution's resiliency and the perennial relevance of *The Federalist* in explaining its constitutionalism offer us hope that we might in future once again put American government on a sounder, more principled footing that will again promote American liberty better than it is being promoted today.

Yet only a Pollyanna would fail to recognize that numerous obstacles stand in the way of such an eventuality. It has become the mantra, for instance, of the intellectual class in America, including many conservatives at the most prominent conservative magazines and think tanks, that the post–New Deal and Great Society welfare state is here to stay; that Americans—especially conservatives—need to exercise "moderation" in their criticism of it because it is both a political necessity and popular; and that to advocate some limited government, natural-right constitutionalism of the variety advocated in *The Federalist* is to indulge a utopianism that was long ago vanquished by history.

To embrace such a mantra is to embrace the very ideology that, in the view of many Americans, is today leading American government into bankruptcy—financial, political, and moral—and that itself may be on the verge of collapse, just another passing ideological fad defended by those who are caught up in the seeming intensity of events. The liberal welfare state is indeed pervasive, and many Americans certainly have become dependent on it, but it is not as entrenched in American politics and the American psyche as many in the chattering classes think. A growing number of citizens, perhaps now an overwhelming majority, see today's liberal welfare state as a dangerous and alien imposition: a form of European state socialism, surreptitiously imposed on Americans by political and cultural elites, that threatens to displace America's natural-rights tradition and the Constitution itself, supplanting these with foreign importations derived from the thinking of Hegel, Marx, Darwin, and Foucault instead of Hamilton, Madison, Washington, and Jefferson.

Threats to the Constitution like these are nothing new in American politics. Both the Constitution and the political science of *The Federalist* have been perennially attacked over America's 220-year history. The extended Union, commercial republicanism, patriotism, greatness, separation of powers, limited government objects, and numerous other features of American constitutionalism originally articulated by *The Federalist* as essential elements of the Constitution so worthy of defense, have come under assault from Anti-Federalists, Calhounites, social Darwinists, pragmatists, Progressives, postmodernists, deconstructionists, multiculturalists, trans-nationalists, and more. Yet the Constitution endures.

So, too, does *The Federalist*, the best guide we have to the meaning of that most fundamental law. As has always been the case, Americans today can turn to the Constitution for guidance in today's politics. And to understand the meaning of the Constitution, they have *The Federalist*, that consummate road map to American constitutionalism, a guide to the future as much as it is to the past—precisely what Publius anticipated.

In the Preface to *The Federalist*, Publius proclaimed that his "great wish" was that the work might "promote the cause of truth and lead to a right judgment of the true interests of the community.[69] In *Federalist* 34, Publius further admonished that when examining the Constitution:

> [It was crucial to] bear in mind that we are not to confine our view to the present period, but to look forward to remote futurity. Constitutions of civil government are not to be framed upon a calculation of existing exigencies, but upon a com-

69. *The Federalist*, Preface, p. lix.

bination of these with the probable exigencies of ages, according to the natural and tried course of human affairs. (*34:175*)

The teaching of *The Federalist* was intended to be true for all times and all places—or at least those places that are ripe for republican government. As the most comprehensive and cogent account of the Founders' natural-rights, limited-government constitutionalism, it demonstrated to us how the Constitution combined the best that ancient and modern political philosophy had to offer: that the Constitution was built upon the enduring principles of the Declaration of Independence, expressing, reconciling, and protecting those principles in new instrumentalities that could persist through time if understood and defended.

In the face of today's ideological threats, the Declaration, the Constitution, and *The Federalist* are still beacons to which Americans can turn for the Founders' natural-rights principles and comprehensive justice.

USEFUL QUOTATIONS
FROM *THE FEDERALIST*

ADMINISTRATION (*SEE EXECUTIVE BRANCH*)

CIVIC VIRTUE

"As there is a degree of depravity in mankind which requires a certain degree of circumspection and distrust: So there are other qualities in human nature, which justify a certain portion of esteem and confidence. Republican government presupposes the existence of these qualities in a higher degree than any other form." ~ *Federalist* 55 (Madison)

"Were the pictures which have been drawn by the political jealousy of some among us, faithful likenesses of the human character, the inference would be that there is not sufficient virtue among men for self-government; and that nothing less than the chains of despotism can restrain them from destroying and devouring each other." ~ *Federalist* 55 (Madison)

"Happy will it be for ourselves, and most honorable for human nature, if we have wisdom and virtue enough to set so glorious an example to mankind!" ~ *Federalist* 36 (Hamilton)

"In a nation of philosophers…reverence for the laws, would be sufficiently inculcated by the voice of an enlightened reason. But a nation of philosophers is as little to be expected as the philosophical race of kings wished for by Plato. And in every other nation, the most rational government will not find it a superfluous advantage, to have the prejudices of the community on its side." ~ *Federalist* 49 (Madison)

"It has been frequently remarked that it seems to have been reserved to the people of this country, by their conduct and example, to decide the important question, whether societies of men are really capable or not of establishing good government from reflection and choice, or whether they are forever destined to depend for their political constitutions on accident and force." ~ *Federalist* I (Hamilton)

CONSENT/SELF-GOVERNMENT

"The fabric of American empire ought to rest on the solid basis of THE CONSENT OF THE PEOPLE. The streams of national power ought to flow from that pure, original fountain of all legitimate authority." ~ *Federalist* 22 (Hamilton)

CONSTITUTIONALISM
(*SEE ALSO RULE OF LAW, SEPARATION OF POWERS*)

"The important distinction so well understood in America between a constitution established by the people, and unalterable by the government; and a law established by the government, and alterable by the government, seems to have been little understood and less observed in any other country." ~ *Federalist* 53 (Madison)

"Tyranny has perhaps oftener grown out of the assumptions of power, called for, on pressing exigencies, by a defective constitution, than out of the full exercise of the largest constitutional authorities." ~ *Federalist* 20 (Hamilton and Madison)

"Every act of a delegated authority, contrary to the tenor of the commission under which it is exercised, is void. No legislative act therefore contrary to the constitution can be valid." ~ *Federalist* 78 (Hamilton)

"In disquisitions of every kind there are certain primary truths, or first principles, upon which all subsequent reasoning must depend." ~ *Federalist* 31 (Hamilton)

"The aim of every political Constitution is or ought to be first to obtain for rulers, men who possess most wisdom to discern, and most virtue to pursue the common good of the society; and in the next place, to take the most effectual precautions for keeping them virtuous, whilst they continue to hold their public trust.... The most effectual one is such a limitation of the term of appointments, as will maintain a proper responsibility to the people." ~ *Federalist* 57 (Madison)

"The Constitution ought to be the standard of construction for the laws, and that wherever there is an evident opposition, the laws ought to give place to the Constitution. But this doctrine is not deducible from any circumstance peculiar to the plan of the convention;

but from the general theory of a limited Constitution."
~ *Federalist* 81 (Hamilton)

DEMAGOGUES

"Of those men who have overturned the liberties of republics, the greatest number have begun their career by paying an obsequious court to the people, commencing demagogues and ending tyrants." ~ *Federalist* 1 (Hamilton)

"There are particular moments in public affairs, when the people stimulated by some irregular passion, or some illicit advantage, or misled by the artful misrepresentations of interested men, may call for measures which they themselves will afterwards be the most ready to lament and condemn." ~ *Federalist* 63 (Madison)

DEMOCRACY

"Democracies have ever been spectacles of turbulence and contention; have ever been found incompatible with personal security, or the rights of property; and have, in general, been as short in their lives as they have been violent in their deaths." ~ *Federalist* 10 (Madison)

"The two great points of difference between a democracy and a republic are, first, the delegation of the government, in the latter, to a small number of citizens elected by the rest; secondly, the greater number of citizens, and the greater sphere of country, over which the latter may be extended." ~ *Federalist* 10 (Madison)

ECONOMIC FREEDOM

"The apportionment of taxes on the various descriptions of property is an act which seems to require the most exact impartiality; yet there is, perhaps, no legislative act in which greater opportunity and temptation are given to a predominant party to trample on the rules of justice. Every shilling which they overburden the inferior number is a shilling saved to their own pockets."
~ *Federalist* 10 (Madison)

"It is evident from the state of the country, from the habits of the people, from the experience we have had on the point itself, that it is impracticable to raise any very considerable sums by direct taxation." ~ *Federalist* 12 (Hamilton)

"If duties are too high, they lessen the consumption; the collection is eluded; and the product to the treasury is not so great as when they are confined within proper and moderate bounds. This forms a complete barrier against any material oppression of the citizens by taxes of this class, and is itself a natural limitation of the power of imposing them." ~ *Federalist* 21 (Hamilton)

"What prudent merchant will hazard his fortunes in any new branch of commerce, when he knows not but that his plans may be rendered unlawful before they can be executed?" ~ *Federalist* 62 (Madison)

"Every new regulation concerning commerce or revenue, or in any manner affecting the value of the different species of property, presents a new harvest to those who watch the change, and can trace its consequences; a harvest reared not for themselves but by the toils and cares of the great body of their fellow citizens." ~ *Federalist* 62 (Madison)

"In the general course of human nature, a power over a man's substance amounts to a power over his will."
~ *Federalist* 73 (Hamilton)

"It might be demonstrated that the most productive system of finance will always be the least burdensome."
~ *Federalist* 35 (Hamilton)

EXECUTIVE BRANCH

"A feeble executive implies a feeble execution of the government. A feeble execution is but another phrase for a bad execution; and a government ill executed, whatever may be its theory, must be, in practice, a bad government." ~ *Federalist* 70 (Hamilton)

"Energy in the executive is a leading character in the definition of good government. It is essential to the protection of the community against foreign attacks; it is not less essential to the steady administration of the laws; to the protection of property against those irregular and high-handed combinations which sometimes interrupt the ordinary course of justice; to the security of liberty against the enterprises and assaults of ambition, of faction, and of anarchy."
~ *Federalist* 70 (Hamilton)

EXPERIENCE

"Is it not the glory of the people of America, that whilst they have paid a decent regard to the opinions of former times and other nations, they have not suffered a blind veneration for antiquity, for custom, or for names, to overrule the suggestions of their own good sense, the knowledge of their own situation, and the lessons of their own experience? To this manly spirit, posterity will be indebted for the possession, and the world for the example of the numerous innovations displayed on the American theatre, in favor of private rights and public happiness." ~ *Federalist* 14 (Madison)

"Experience is the oracle of truth; and where its responses are unequivocal, they ought to be conclusive and sacred." ~ *Federalist* 20 (Hamilton and Madison)

"That experience is the parent of wisdom is an adage, the truth of which is recognized by the wisest as well as the simplest of mankind." ~ *Federalist* 72 (Hamilton)

"They accomplished a revolution which has no parallel in the annals of human society. They reared the fabrics of governments which have no model on the face of the globe. They formed the design of a great Confederacy, which it is incumbent on their successors to improve and perpetuate." ~ *Federalist* 14 (Madison)

FACTION

"The inference to which we are brought is, that the *causes* of faction cannot be removed, and that relief is only to be sought in the means of controlling its *effects*." ~ *Federalist* 10 (Madison)

"Extend the sphere and you take in a greater variety of parties and interests; you make it less probable that a majority of the whole will have common motive to invade the rights of other citizens." ~ *Federalist* 10 (Madison)

"In a society under the forms of which the stronger faction can readily unite and oppress the weaker, anarchy may as truly be said to reign as in a state of nature."
~ *Federalist* 51 (Madison)

"The latent causes of faction are thus sown in the nature of man." ~ *Federalist* 10 (Madison)

"By a faction I understand a number of citizens, whether amounting to a majority or minority of the whole, who are united and actuated by some common impulse of passion, or of interest, adverse to the rights of other citizens, or to the permanent and aggregate interests of the community." ~ *Federalist* 10 (Madison)

FEDERALISM

"The Federal Constitution forms a happy combination in this respect; the great and aggregate interests being referred to the national, the local and particular to the state legislatures." ~ *Federalist* 10 (Madison)

"It is to be remembered, that the general government is not to be charged with the whole power of making and administering laws. Its jurisdiction is limited to certain enumerated objects, which concern all the members of the public, but which are not to be obtained by the separate provisions of any. The subordinate governments which can extend their care to all those other objects, which can be separately provided for, will retain their due authority and activity." ~ *Federalist* 14 (Madison)

"The new Constitution will, if established, be a FEDERAL, and not a NATIONAL constitution."
~ *Federalist* 39 (Madison)

"The powers delegated by the proposed Constitution to the federal government are few and defined. Those which are to remain in the State governments are numerous and indefinite." ~ *Federalist* 45 (Madison)

"The proposed Constitution, so far from implying an abolition of the State governments, makes them constituent parts of the national sovereignty, by allowing them a direct representation in the Senate, and leaves in their possessions certain exclusive and very important portions of sovereign power. This fully corresponds, in every rational import of the terms, with the idea of a federal government." ~ *Federalist* 9 (Hamilton)

FOREIGN AFFAIRS (*SEE ALSO HUMAN NATURE, NATIONAL SECURITY AND WAR*)

"Let us recollect that peace or war will not always be left to our option; that however moderate or unambitious we may be, we cannot count upon the moderation, or hope to extinguish the ambition of others." ~ *Federalist* 34 (Hamilton)

"When the sword is once drawn, the passions of men observe no bounds of moderation." ~ *Federalist* 16 (Hamilton)

"To judge from the history of mankind, we shall be compelled to conclude, that the fiery and destructive passions of war reign in the human breast with much more powerful sway, than the mild and beneficent systems of peace; and that to model our political systems upon speculations of lasting tranquility, is to calculate on the weaker springs of human character." ~ *Federalist* 34 (Hamilton)

"Security against foreign danger is one of the primitive objects of civil society." ~ *Federalist* 41 (Madison)

"How could a readiness for war in time of peace be safely prohibited, unless we could prohibit, in like manner, the preparations and establishments of every hostile nation?" ~ *Federalist* 41 (Madison)

GOVERNMENT POWER (*SEE ALSO SEPARATION OF POWERS*)

"It will be forgotten, on the one hand, that jealousy is the usual concomitant of violent love, and that the noble enthusiasm of liberty is too apt to be infected with a spirit of narrow and illiberal distrust. On the other hand, it will be equally forgotten, that the vigour of government is essential to the security of liberty." ~ *Federalist* 1 (Hamilton)

"The circumstances that endanger the safety of nations are infinite, and for this reason no constitutional shackles can wisely be imposed on the power to which the care of it is committed." ~ *Federalist* 23 (Hamilton)

"The accumulation of all powers, legislative, executive, and judiciary, in the same hands, whether of one, a few, or many, and whether hereditary, self-appointed, or elective, may justly be pronounced the very definition of tyranny." ~ *Federalist* 48 (Madison)

HUMAN NATURE (*SEE ALSO CIVIC VIRTUE*)

"Has it not, on the contrary, invariably been found, that momentary passions and immediate interests have a more active and imperious control over human conduct than general or remote considerations of policy, utility, or justice? Have republics in practice been less addicted to war than monarchies? Are not the former administered by men as well as the latter?" ~ *Federalist* 6 (Hamilton)

"Why has government been instituted at all? Because the passions of men will not conform to the dictates of reason and justice, without constraint. Has it been found that bodies of men act with more rectitude or greater disinterestedness than individuals? The contrary of this has been inferred by all accurate observers of the conduct of mankind." ~ *Federalist* 15 (Hamilton)

"But the mild voice of reason, pleading the cause of an enlarged and permanent interest, is but too often drowned before public bodies as well as individuals, by the clamours of an impatient avidity for immediate and immoderate gain." ~ *Federalist* 42 (Madison)

"Ambition must be made to counteract ambition. The interest of the man must be connected with the constitutional rights of the place. It may be a reflection on human nature that such devices should be necessary to control the abuses of government. But what is government itself but the greatest of all reflections on human nature? If men were angels, no government would be necessary. If angels were to govern men, neither external nor internal controls on government would be necessary." ~ *Federalist* 51 (Madison)

"It is a general principle of human nature, that a man will be interested in whatever he possesses, in proportion to the firmness or precariousness of the tenure, by which he holds it; will be less attached to what he holds by a momentary or uncertain title." ~ *Federalist* 71 (Hamilton)

"Men are ambitious, vindictive, and rapacious. To look for a continuation of harmony between a number of independent unconnected sovereignties, situated in the same neighborhood, would be to disregard the uniform course of events, and to set at defiance the accumulated experience of ages." ~ *Federalist* 6 (Hamilton)

"The reason of man, like man himself is timid and cautious, when left alone; and acquires firmness and confidence, in proportion to the number with which it is associated." ~ *Federalist* 49 (Madison)

"The desire of reward is one of the strongest incentives of human conduct.... [T]he best security for the fidelity of mankind is to make their interest coincide with their duty." ~ *Federalist* 72 (Hamilton)

JUDICIARY

"If, then, the courts of justice are to be considered as the bulwarks of a limited Constitution against legislative encroachments, this consideration will afford a strong argument for the permanent tenure of judicial offices, since nothing will contribute so much as this to that independent spirit in the judges which must be essential to the faithful performance of so arduous a duty." ~ *Federalist* 78 (Hamilton)

"Whoever attentively considers the different departments of power must perceive, that, in a government in which they are separated from each other, the judiciary, from the nature of its functions, will always be the least dangerous to the political rights of the Constitution; because it will be least in a capacity to annoy or injure them." ~ *Federalist* 78 (Hamilton)

"As liberty can have nothing to fear from the judiciary alone, but would have everything to fear from its union with either of the other departments." ~ *Federalist* 78 (Hamilton)

"The interpretation of the laws is the proper and peculiar province of the courts. A constitution is, in fact, and must be regarded by the judges, as a fundamental law. It therefore belongs to them to ascertain its meaning as well as the meaning of any other act proceeding from the legislative body. If there should happen to be an irreconcilable variance between the two, that which has the superior obligation and validity ought of course to be preferred; or in other words, the constitution ought to be preferred to the statute, the intention of the people to the intention of their agents." ~ *Federalist* 78 (Hamilton)

"The judiciary...has no influence over either the sword or the purse, no direction either of the strength or of the wealth of the society, and can take no active resolution whatever. It may be truly said to have neither force nor will, but merely judgment; and must ultimately depend upon the aid of the executive arm even for the efficacy of its judgments." ~ *Federalist* 78 (Hamilton)

LEGISLATIVE BRANCH

"The legislative department is everywhere extending the sphere of its activity, and drawing all power into its impetuous vortex." ~ *Federalist* 48 (Madison)

"The number [of legislators] ought at most to be kept within a certain limit, in order to avoid the confusion and intemperance of a multitude. In all very numerous assemblies, of whatever characters composed, passion never fails to wrest the scepter from reason. Had every Athenian citizen been a Socrates; every Athenian assembly would still have been a mob." ~ *Federalist* 55 (Madison)

"In the legislature, promptitude of decision is oftener an evil than a benefit. The differences of opinion, and the jarrings of parties in that department of government, though they may sometimes obstruct salutary plans, yet often promote deliberation and circumspection; and serve to check excesses in the majority." ~ *Federalist* 70 (Hamilton)

"What is to restrain the House of Representatives from making legal discriminations in favor of themselves and a particular class of the society? I answer, the genius of the whole system, the nature of just and constitutional laws, and above all the vigilant and manly spirit which actuates the people of America, a spirit which nourishes freedom, and in return is nourished by it. If this spirit shall ever be so debased as to tolerate a law not obligatory on the legislature as well as on the people, the people will be prepared to tolerate anything but liberty." ~ *Federalist* 57 (Madison)

"Enlightened statesmen will not always be at the helm." ~ *Federalist* 10 (Madison)

"The house of representatives...can make no law which will not have its full operation on themselves and their friends, as well as the great mass of society. This has always been deemed one of the strongest bonds by which human policy can connect the rulers and the people together. It creates between them that communion of interest, and sympathy of sentiments, of which few governments have furnished examples; but without which every government degenerates into tyranny." ~ *Federalist* 57 (Madison)

"The people can never willfully betray their own interests: But they may possibly be betrayed by the representatives of the people; and the danger will be evidently greater where the whole legislative trust is lodged in the hands of one body of men, than where the concurrence of separate and dissimilar bodies is required in every public act." ~ *Federalist* 63 (Madison)

"The effect of [representation] is, on the one hand to refine and enlarge the public views, by passing them through the medium of a chosen body of citizens, whose wisdom may best discern the true interest of their country, and whose patriotism and love of justice, will be least likely to sacrifice it to temporary or partial considerations." ~ *Federalist* 10 (Madison)

"The people can never err more than in supposing that by multiplying their representatives, beyond a certain limit, they strengthen the barrier against the government of a few. Experience will forever admonish them that on the contrary, after securing a sufficient number for the purposes of safety, of local information, and of diffusive sympathy with the whole society, they will counteract their own views by every addition to their representatives. The countenance of the government may become more democratic; but the soul that animates it will be more oligarchic." ~ *Federalist* 58 (Madison)

"No man can be a competent legislator who does not add to an upright intention and a sound judgment, a certain degree of knowledge of the subjects on which he is to legislate." ~ *Federalist* 53 (Madison)

"In republican government the legislative authority, necessarily, dominates. The remedy for this inconveniency is, to divide the legislature into different branches." ~ *Federalist* 51 (Madison)

"When occasions present themselves in which the interests of the people are at variance with their inclinations, it is the duty of the persons whom they have appointed to be the guardians of those interests to withstand the temporary delusion in order to give them time and opportunity for more cool and sedate reflection." ~ *Federalist* 71 (Hamilton)

LIBERTY/LIMITED GOVERNMENT

"The injury which may possibly be done by defeating a few good laws, will be amply compensated by the advantage of preventing a number of bad ones." ~ *Federalist* 73 (Hamilton)

"Liberty is to faction what air is to fire, an aliment without which it instantly expires. But it could not be less folly to abolish liberty, which is essential to political life, because it nourishes faction, than it would be to wish the annihilation of air, which is essential to animal life, because it imparts to fire its destructive agency." ~ *Federalist* 10 (Madison)

"It will not be denied that power is of an encroaching nature and that it ought to be effectually restrained from passing the limits assigned to it." ~ *Federalist* 48 (Madison)

"In a free government the security for civil rights must be the same as that for religious rights." ~ *Federalist* 51 (Madison)

"If the federal government should overpass the just bounds of its authority and make a tyrannical use of its powers, the people, whose creature it is, must appeal to the standard they have formed, and take such measures to redress the injury done to the Constitution as the exigency may suggest and prudence justify." ~ *Federalist* 33 (Hamilton)

"Liberty may be endangered by the abuses of liberty, as well as by the abuses of power." ~ *Federalist* 63 (Madison)

"The regular distribution of power into distinct departments; the introduction of legislative balances and checks; the institution of courts composed of judges holding their offices during good behavior; the representation of the people in the legislature by deputies of their own election... They are means, and powerful means, by which the excellences of republican government may be retained and its imperfections lessened or avoided." ~ *Federalist* 9 (Hamilton)

"One hundred and seventy-three despots would surely be as oppressive as one." ~ *Federalist* 48 (Madison)

"In framing a government which is to be administered by men over men, the great difficulty lies in this: you must first enable the government to control the governed; and in the next place, oblige it to control itself." ~ *Federalist* 51 (Madison)

"The plan of the [constitutional] convention declares that the power of congress or in other words of the national legislature, shall extend to certain enumerated cases. This specification of particulars evidently excludes all pretension to a general legislative authority; because an affirmative grant of powers would be absurd as well as useless, if a general authority was intended." ~ *Federalist* 83 (Hamilton)

NATIONAL SECURITY AND WAR (*SEE ALSO FOREIGN AFFAIRS*)

"The authorities essential to the common defense are these: to raise armies; to build and equip fleets; to prescribe rules for the government of both; to direct their operations; to provide for their support. These powers ought to exist without limitation, *because it is impossible to foresee or to define the extent and variety of national exigencies, and the correspondent extent and variety of the means which may be necessary to satisfy them.* The circumstances that endanger the safety of nations are infinite, and for this reason no constitutional shackles can wisely be imposed on the power to which the care of it is committed. This power ought to be coextensive with all the possible combinations of such circumstances; and ought to be under the direction of the same councils which are appointed to preside over the common defense." ~ *Federalist* 23 (Hamilton; emphasis in original)

"The means of security can only be regulated by the means and the danger of attack. They will, in fact, be ever determined by these rules and by no others. It is in vain to oppose constitutional barriers to the impulse of self-preservation. It is worse than in vain; because it plants in the Constitution itself necessary usurpations of power, every precedent of which is a germ of unnecessary and multiplied repetitions. If one nation main-tains constantly a disciplined army, ready for the service of ambition or revenge, it obliges the most pacific nations who may be within the reach of its enterprises to take corresponding precautions." ~ *Federalist* 41 (Madison)

"Of all the cares or concerns of government, the direction of war most peculiarly demands those qualities which distinguish the exercise of power by a single hand. The direction of war implies the direction of the common strength; and the power of directing and employing the common strength forms a usual and essential part in the definition of the executive authority." ~ *Federalist* 74 (Hamilton)

"War, like most other things, is a science to be acquired and perfected by diligence, by perseverance, by time, and by practice." ~ *Federalist* 26 (Hamilton)

"The means of revenue, which have been so greatly multiplied by the increase of gold and silver and of the arts of industry, and the science of finance, which is the offspring of modern times, concurring with the habits of nations, have produced an entire revolution in the system of war, and have rendered disciplined armies, distinct from the body of the citizens, the inseparable companion of frequent hostility." ~ *Federalist* 8 (Hamilton)

"The rights of neutrality will only be respected when they are defended by an adequate power. A nation, des-picable by its weakness, forfeits even the privilege of being neutral." ~ *Federalist* 11 (Hamilton)

PARTISAN POLITICS (*SEE ALSO HUMAN NATURE*)

"For in politics, as in religion, it is equally absurd to aim at making proselytes by fire and sword. Heresies in either can rarely be cured by persecution." ~ *Federalist* I (Hamilton)

"Ambition, avarice, personal animosity, party opposition, and many other motives not more laudable than these, are apt to operate as well upon those who support as those who oppose the right side of a question." ~ *Federalist* I (Hamilton)

"It is a misfortune, inseparable from human affairs, that public measures are rarely investigated with that spirit of moderation which is essential to a just estimate of their real tendency to advance or obstruct the public good; and that this spirit is more apt to be diminished than prompted, by those occasions which require an unusual exercise of it." ~ *Federalist* 37 (Madison)

PATRIOTISM

"It is impossible for the man of pious reflection not to perceive in [the Constitution] a finger of that Almighty hand which has been so frequently and signally extended to our relief in the critical stages of the revolution." ~ *Federalist* 37 (Madison)

"Every man who loves peace, every man who loves his country, every man who loves liberty, ought to have it ever before his eyes that he may cherish in his heart a due attachment to the Union of America, and be able to set a due value on the means of preserving it." ~ *Federalist* 41 (Madison)

PROGRESS AND UTOPIANISM

"I never expect to see a perfect work from imperfect man." ~ *Federalist* 85 (Hamilton)

"If mankind were to resolve to agree in no institution of government, until every part of it had been adjusted to the most exact standard of perfection, society would soon become a general scene of anarchy, and the world a desert." ~ *Federalist* 65 (Hamilton)

"Is it not time to awake from the deceitful dream of a golden age, and to adopt as a practical maxim for the direction of our political conduct, that we, as well as the other inhabitants of the globe, are yet remote from the happy empire of perfect wisdom and perfect virtue?" ~ *Federalist* 6 (Hamilton)

"The purest of human blessings must have a portion of alloy in them, that the choice must always be made, if not of the lesser evil, at least of the greater, not the perfect good." ~ *Federalist* 41 (Madison)

PURPOSE OF GOVERNMENT

"Justice is the end of government. It is the end of civil society. It ever has been and ever will be pursued until it be obtained, or until liberty be lost in the pursuit." ~ *Federalist* 51 (Madison)

"The diversity in the faculties of men from which the rights of property originate, is not less an insuperable obstacle to a uniformity of interests. The protection of these faculties is the first object of government" ~ *Federalist* 10 (Madison)

"It is the reason of the public alone that ought to control and regulate the government. The passions ought to be controlled and regulated by the government."
~ *Federalist* 49 (Madison)

"It is too early for politicians to presume on our forgetting that the public good, the real welfare of the great body of the people, is the supreme object to be pursued; and that no form of government whatever has any other value than as it may be fitted for the attainment of this object." ~ *Federalist* 45 (Madison)

REPUBLICANISM

"The genius of Republican liberty, seems to demand on one side, not only that all power should be derived from the people; but, that those entrusted with it should be kept in dependence on the people, by a short duration of their appointments; and, that, even during this short period, the trust should be placed not in a few, but in a number of hands." ~ *Federalist* 37 (Madison)

"It is of great importance in a republic, not only to guard the society against the oppression of its rulers; but to guard one part of the society against the injustice of the other part." ~ *Federalist* 51 (Madison)

"It is a misfortune incident to republican government, though in a less degree than to other governments, that those who administer it, may forget their obligations to their constituents, and prove unfaithful to their important trust." ~ *Federalist* 62 (Madison)

"The republican principle demands that the deliberate sense of the community should govern the conduct of those to whom they entrust the management of their affairs; but it does not require an unqualified complaisance to every sudden breeze of passion or to every transient impulse which the people may receive from the arts of men, who flatter their prejudices to betray their interests." ~ *Federalist* 71 (Hamilton)

"The natural cure for an ill-administration, in a popular or representative constitution, is a change of men." ~ *Federalist* 21 (Hamilton)

"The first question that offers itself is, whether the general form and aspect of the government be strictly republican? It is evident that no other form would be reconcilable with the genius of the people of America; with the fundamental principles of the revolution; or with that honorable determination, which animates every votary of freedom, to rest all our political experiments on the capacity of mankind for self-government." ~ *Federalist* 39 (Madison)

"We may define a republic to be, or at least may bestow that name on, a government which derives all its powers directly or indirectly from the great body of the people; and is administered by persons holding their offices during pleasure, for a limited period, or during good behaviour." ~ *Federalist* 39 (Madison)

RULE OF LAW (*SEE ALSO JUDICIARY*)

"Wise politicians will be cautious about fettering the government with restrictions that cannot be observed, because they know that every break of the fundamental laws, though dictated by necessity, impairs that sacred reverence which ought to be maintained in the breast of

rulers towards the constitution of a country."
~ *Federalist* 25 (Hamilton)

"It will be of little avail to the people, that the laws are made by men of their own choice, if the laws be so voluminous that they cannot be read, or so incoherent that they cannot be understood; if they be repealed or revised before they are promulgated, or undergo such incessant changes that no man, who knows what the law is to-day, can guess what it will be to-morrow. Law is defined to be a rule of action; but how can that be a rule, which is little known and less fixed?" ~ *Federalist* 62 (Madison)

"As every appeal to the people would carry an implication of some defect in the government, frequent appeals would in great measure deprive the government of that veneration, which time bestows on everything, and without which perhaps the wisest and freest governments would not possess the requisite stability." ~ *Federalist* 49 (Madison)

SEPARATION OF POWERS (*SEE ALSO CONSTITUTIONALISM, GOVERNMENT POWER*)

"It will not be denied that power is of an encroaching nature and that it ought to be effectually restrained from passing the limits assigned to it. After discriminating, therefore, in theory, the several classes of power, as they may in their nature be legislative, executive, or judiciary, the next and most difficult task is to provide some practical security for each, against the invasion of the others." ~ *Federalist* 48 (Madison)

"A dependence on the people is, no doubt, the primary control on the government; but experience has taught mankind the necessity of auxiliary precautions."
~ *Federalist* 51 (Madison)

"The great security against a gradual concentration of the several powers in the same department consists in giving to those who administer each department the necessary constitutional means and personal motives to resist encroachments of the others." ~ *Federalist* 51 (Madison)

SLAVERY

"It were doubtless to be wished that the power of prohibiting the importation of slaves, had not been postponed until the year 1808, or rather that it had been suffered to have immediate operation. But…it ought to be considered as a great point in favor of humanity, that a period of twenty years may terminate for ever within these states, a traffic which has so long and so loudly upbraided the barbarism of modern policy." ~ *Federalist* 42 (Madison)

TAXES (*SEE ECONOMIC FREEDOM*)

VIGILANCE

"For it is a truth which the experience of all ages has attested, that the people are always most in danger, when the means of injuring their rights are in the possession of those of whom they entertain the least suspicion." ~ *Federalist* 25 (Hamilton)